D0241694

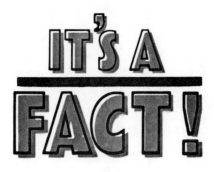

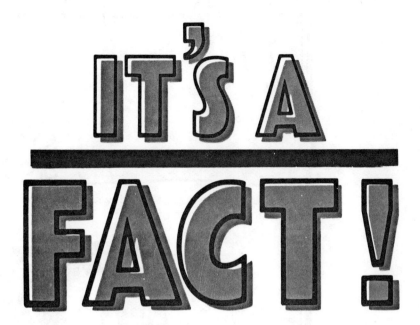

TREASURE PRESS

A great proportion of British women develop bunions by the age of forty.

Henry VIII's second wife, Anne Boleyn, spent the night of her execution in the same room in the Tower of London in which she had spent the night before her coronation.

Rats can survive without water longer than camels.

Sunglasses were first
worn by film stars,
not in an attempt to
look mysterious,
but to relieve their eyes
from the dazzling glare of
the early studio lights.

A litre of vinegar is heavier
in winter than in summer.

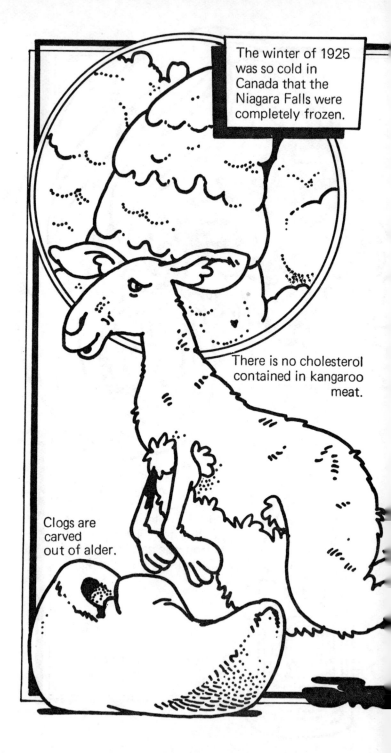

The winter of 1925 was so cold in Canada that the Niagara Falls were completely frozen.

There is no cholesterol contained in kangaroo meat.

Clogs are carved out of alder.

OVER TEN TIMES AS MANY TELEGRAMS ARE SENT IN THE USSR EACH YEAR AS THE NUMBER SENT IN THE USA.

Modern binoculars are more powerful than Galileo's telescope.

As it burns magnesium gains weight and its ashes are heavier than the original piece of metal.

Aborigines were treating wounds with moulds growing on trees, thousands of years before the discovery of penicillin.

Great Danes were first bred in Germany and have nothing to do with Denmark, except for their English names.

Crocuses have been known to force their way through tarmac.

Monkeys native to the American continent have prehensile tails that they use for climbing. However, their cousins in other parts of the world are less fortunate and cannot use their tails for this purpose.

Giuseppe Verdi was commissioned to write his opera 'Aida' to commemorate the opening of the Suez Canal.

The fearless Prussian commander whose timely arrival sealed Napoleon's defeat had one constant phobia. Blucher lived in dread of giving birth to an elephant.

Every day for three or four months every bottle of champagne is gently shaken to make the sediment settle on the end of the cork, before the wine can be fully cleared.

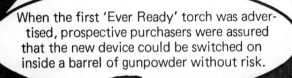

When the first 'Ever Ready' torch was adver-
tised, prospective purchasers were assured
that the new device could be switched on
inside a barrel of gunpowder without risk.

In Cuba the
natives believe
that walking
around in the
moonlight with
a bare head is
asking for
trouble. The
light of the moon
has many disas-
trous and evil
effects — in Cuba
at least.

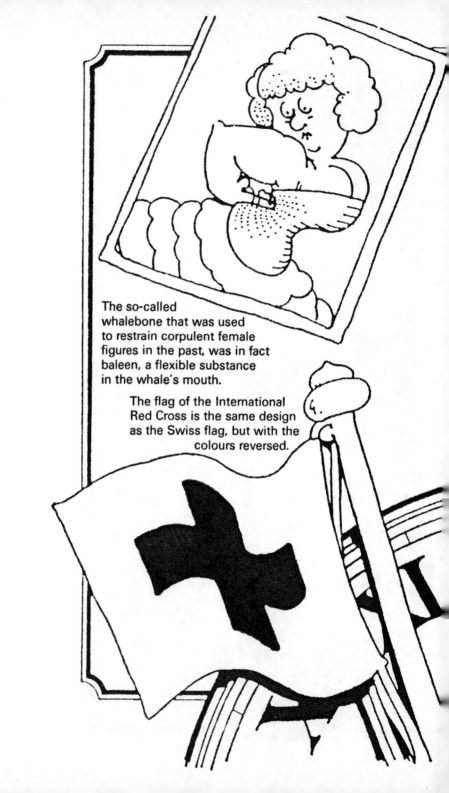

The so-called whalebone that was used to restrain corpulent female figures in the past, was in fact baleen, a flexible substance in the whale's mouth.

The flag of the International Red Cross is the same design as the Swiss flag, but with the colours reversed.

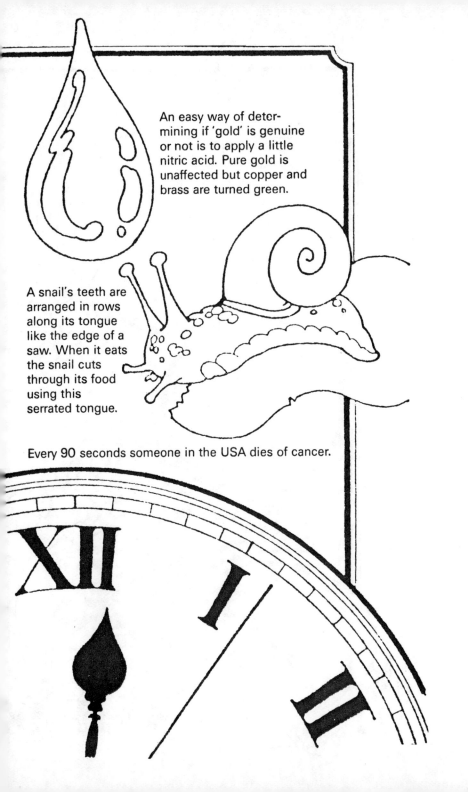

An easy way of determining if 'gold' is genuine or not is to apply a little nitric acid. Pure gold is unaffected but copper and brass are turned green.

A snail's teeth are arranged in rows along its tongue like the edge of a saw. When it eats the snail cuts through its food using this serrated tongue.

Every 90 seconds someone in the USA dies of cancer.

The onion is named after the Latin word 'unio' which means 'a large pearl'.

The British government offered a reward of £5,000 in 1776 to anyone who could discover the North West Passage.

Both King Constantine of Greece and King Olav of Norway won Olympic gold medals for sailing.

There is a town called Oo in the departement of Haute Garonne, in south-west France.

15

Oaks and Poplars are struck by lightning more frequently than any other trees in England.

Over thirty states in the USA produce petrol.

Over 95 per cent of fifteen year olds have already developed some decay in their permanent teeth.

In spite of its ungainly appearance the giraffe can usually outrun most of its predators.

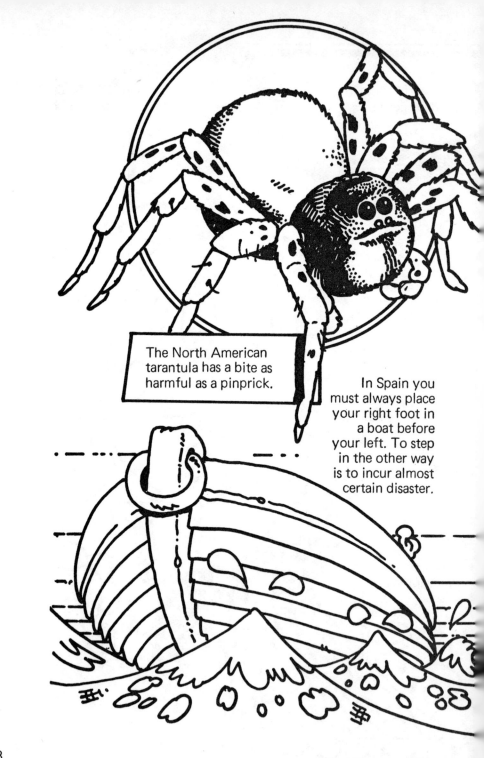

The North American tarantula has a bite as harmful as a pinprick.

In Spain you must always place your right foot in a boat before your left. To step in the other way is to incur almost certain disaster.

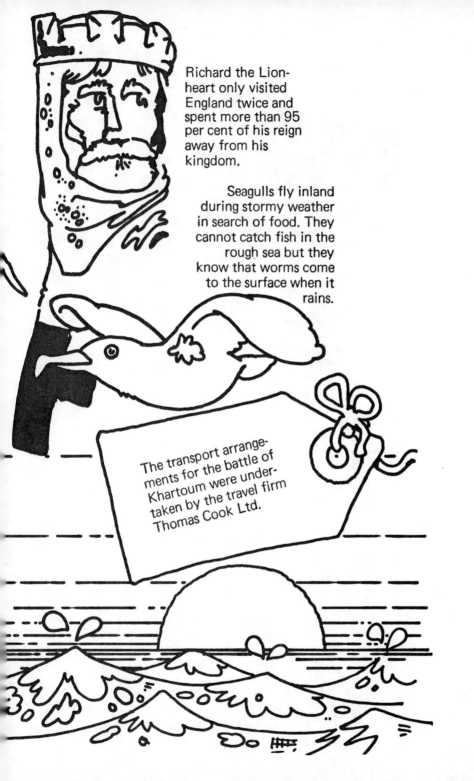

Richard the Lion-heart only visited England twice and spent more than 95 per cent of his reign away from his kingdom.

Seagulls fly inland during stormy weather in search of food. They cannot catch fish in the rough sea but they know that worms come to the surface when it rains.

The transport arrangements for the battle of Khartoum were undertaken by the travel firm Thomas Cook Ltd.

Rembrandt's famous painting 'Night Watch' was received by its original commissioners, the Dutch Civic Guard, with mixed feelings. Many of them were very disappointed with the painting.

Pliny the Elder, author of his famous 37-volume 'Historia Naturalis', mentioned a cure for corns which entailed the patient gazing fixedly into the heavens while oil was poured on to a door hinge.

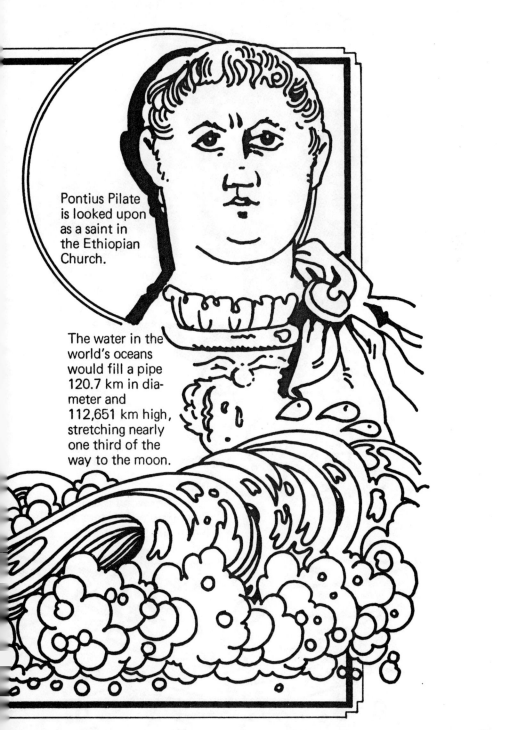

Pontius Pilate is looked upon as a saint in the Ethiopian Church.

The water in the world's oceans would fill a pipe 120.7 km in diameter and 112,651 km high, stretching nearly one third of the way to the moon.

The planet Uranus can only just be seen by the naked eye.

Early golf balls used to be made with leather bags stuffed with feathers.

Boxwood is one of the few woods that actually sinks in water.

The daily outflow of the Amazon would be enough to supply the USA with two hundred times its daily municipal water requirement.

In the past most fishes were covered with protective armour.

In June 1969 stowaway Socarras Ramirez escaped from Cuba to Spain in a wing cavity of an airliner. He survived the 9,000 km journey at an altitude of over 9,000 m in temperatures of -22°C.

Napoleon Bonaparte designed the Italian flag.

Asses, horses and zebras all clean themselves in an unconventional way — they roll in dust.

The greatest number of people to be piled on top of a pillar box is twenty-nine.

The only times when there are an equal number of hours of light and dark everywhere on earth are at the equinoxes in March and September.

Medical studies into cold viruses have shown that more people catch colds by holding hands than by kissing.

German strongman Siegmund Breitbart was able to bite through 5mm thick steel bars, break chains by expanding his chest, and could push large nails through iron with his bare fist.

In one of his portraits of Charles I Van Dyck painted the king wearing his full armour and carrying two gauntlets, both for his right hand.

On the Caribbean island of Haiti the local buses are called 'Tap-Taps' because of the noise made by their diesel engines.

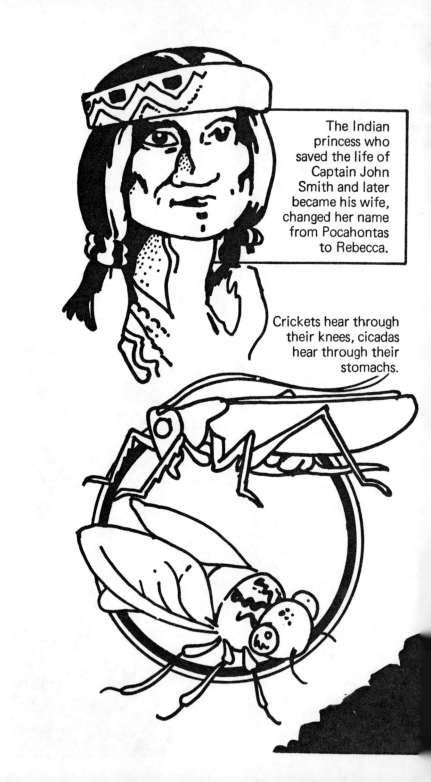

The Indian princess who saved the life of Captain John Smith and later became his wife, changed her name from Pocahontas to Rebecca.

Crickets hear through their knees, cicadas hear through their stomachs.

John Dryden's brother-in-law was one of the many late 17th century and 18th century dramatists who rewrote Shakespeare's plays. In his version of 'Romeo and Juliet' the 'star-crossed lovers' live happily ever after.

In strict medical terms morons are more intelligent than imbeciles, who in turn are more intelligent than idiots.

One tonne of uranium produces the same amount of energy as 30,000 tonnes of coal.

A law in the state of Ohio, USA, requires domestic animals that are out after lighting-up time to wear taillights.

The dollar sign is a modified version of the figure eight which used to be stamped on the old Spanish 'pieces of eight'.

Spain is named after the Carthaginian word meaning 'land of rabbits'.

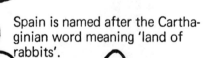

The response of the British Admiralty to the invention of the submarine in the early 17th century was that it was 'a damn silly, trifling novelty that will never catch on'.

The ancient city of Troy was probably a large village that covered an area of about three hectares.

Jacobite supporters in the early 18th century used to give a toast to 'the gentleman in black velvet'. This was in fact the mole, who built the molehill which caused William III's horse to stumble, and the king to fall and subsequently die.

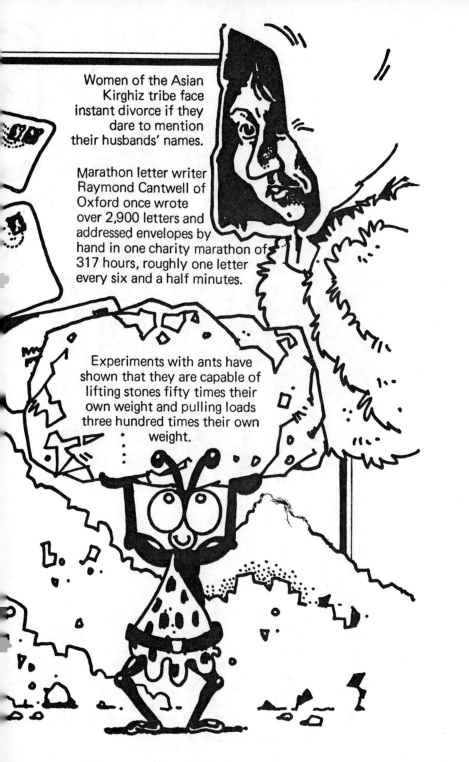

Women of the Asian Kirghiz tribe face instant divorce if they dare to mention their husbands' names.

Marathon letter writer Raymond Cantwell of Oxford once wrote over 2,900 letters and addressed envelopes by hand in one charity marathon of 317 hours, roughly one letter every six and a half minutes.

Experiments with ants have shown that they are capable of lifting stones fifty times their own weight and pulling loads three hundred times their own weight.

Tomatoes were originally called 'love apples'.

The water drawn up by artesian wells in Australia fell as rain 6,000 years ago.

The planet Uranus was originally named after George III 'Georgium Sidium'. It was not named after the Roman god until 1850.

Most mammals are unable to perceive colours and are limited to 'black and white' vision; only the higher apes like chimpanzees and some monkeys share man's colour vision.

Ludwig van Beethoven believed that his brain was stimulated if he poured ice cold water over his head while he was working.

The price of coffee today, compared with the overall cost of living, is roughly the same as it was in the late 17th century.

If you have an
I.Q. of 180 or
over you are
literally one
person in a
million.

Horses show aggression by
laying back their ears.

The winter of 1592 was so cold that starving wolves dared to enter Vienna and attacked both men and livestock.

The USA had no national anthem until 1931.

One of the candidates who failed at his first attempt to pass the entrance examinations for the Federal Polytechnic of Zurich was a young man called Albert Einstein.

Ancient Chinese belief held that sperm came from the brain.

Some of the dams built by beavers are as much as fifteen metres long.

Polar bears can outrun reindeer
and could probably beat an
Olympic champion swimmer over a long
distance
swim.

The first man to be
imprisoned for a
traffic offence was
ironically the first
motorist Nicholas
Cugnot, who drove
his steam-powered
tractor into a stone
wall, at the top speed
of six and a half
kilometres an hour.

Commenting on President Lincoln's famous words from the Gettysburg address, 'Government of the people, by the people, and for the people', the London Times remarked, 'Anything more dull and commonplace it would not be easy to reproduce.'

The necklaces of flowers that are so often seen in photographs of the Pacific islands are very intricate to make. Many of them contain 450 flowers or more.

Before being shot by a big game hunter in 1911, a tigress in Northern India had been killing the local population at an average of just over one human a week, for the last eight years.

Among the sports considered to be unsuitable for Sunday recreation during the reign of James I were bear-baiting, short plays and mimes, and bowling.

Only one quarter of the amount of plants grow on land each year as grow in the ocean.

Crows are able to distinguish a man with a gun from one without.

An American was granted a divorce by a court in the state of Maine on the grounds that his wife had forced him to live exclusively on a diet of pea soup.

Annie Oakley could shoot a hole in a playing card tossed into the air.

Big Ben was slowed by five minutes one day in 1945 when a passing group of starlings decided to take a rest on the minute hand of the clock.

The Danish astronomer Tycho Brahe, who wore an artificial nose of gold and silver, always carried a small box of glue wherever he went in case the nose became loose.

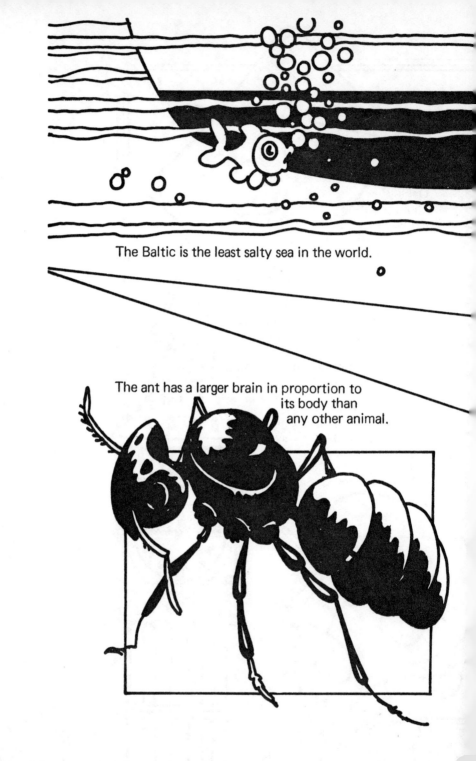

The Baltic is the least salty sea in the world.

The ant has a larger brain in proportion to its body than any other animal.

A ship's hull collects a hundred tonnes of barnacles every year.

The British tennis player Mike Sangster served a tennis ball in June 1963 that moved at 247.8 km/h.

Sarah Bernhardt had a wooden leg in later life.

Volleyball is the most popular sport played in American nudist camps.

In parts of North Africa the native Arabs call out 'Iron, iron' whenever a storm threatens to break. They believe that the evil spirits that caused the storm are scared off by the metal.

The ideal American diet would kill a monkey in a comparatively short time.

Shamefully conscious of his baldness and humiliated by the jokes at his expense, Czar Paul I of Russia decreed that anyone who mentioned his condition in his presence would be liable to be flogged to death.

The name of the African state of Sierra Leone means 'Lion Mountain'.

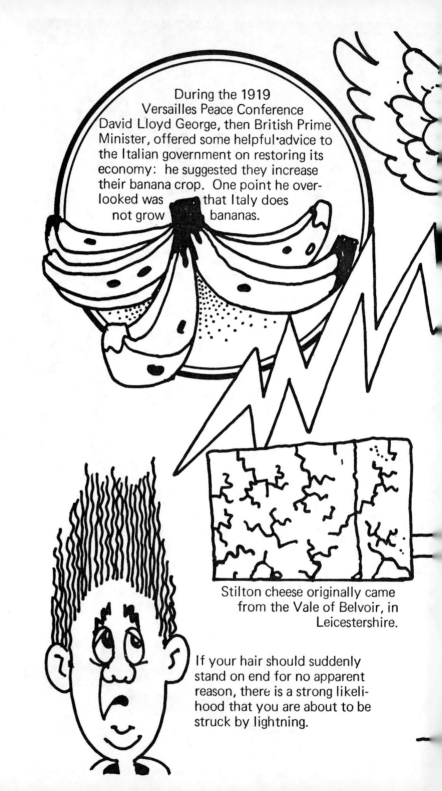

During the 1919 Versailles Peace Conference David Lloyd George, then British Prime Minister, offered some helpful advice to the Italian government on restoring its economy: he suggested they increase their banana crop. One point he overlooked was that Italy does not grow bananas.

Stilton cheese originally came from the Vale of Belvoir, in Leicestershire.

If your hair should suddenly stand on end for no apparent reason, there is a strong likelihood that you are about to be struck by lightning.

Apart from Lucifer,
the fallen angel,
Gabriel and Michael
are the only angels
mentioned by name
in the Bible.

Royal gossip enthusiasts assert that
the Duke of Edinburgh has been
known to attend Royal Ascot with
a transistor radio concealed under
his top hat, so that he could listen
to the cricket commentary.

In 1887 the famous French Post-
Impressionist painter, Paul
Gauguin, worked on the Panama
Canal.

The sight of the first top hat to be worn in London caused such public alarm that the wearer was called to appear before the Lord Mayor and bound over to keep the peace for £50.

On the island of Pitcairn, in the Pacific, it is against the law to shout 'sail ho', when there is no ship to be seen.

Ice Age glaciers were responsible for covering ten per cent of the earth's surface with their debris.

The Tuatara is the last survivor of an order of reptiles that inhabited the earth 250,000,000 years ago. Today it only lives in parts of New Zealand and its eggs take a year or more to incubate.

During the First World War it was reported that the Kaiser had demanded a performance of 'The Merry Wives of Saxe-Coburg and Gotha' after King George V had changed his surname to Windsor.

A Hammer

The Brain

The Head

The brain is incapable of feeling pain. Headaches come from the muscles and nerves that surround the brain, not from the brain itself.

The most popular insects eaten by the people of different cultures around the world, are grasshoppers, beetles, crickets, locusts, caterpillars, termites and ants.

When Igor Stravinsky's ballet 'The Rite of Spring' received its first performance there was a riot. The audience was appalled by the unconventional nature of the work and Stravinsky had to escape out of a window back-stage.

The word 'flak', used to describe anti-aircraft fire, is a compression of the German word for 'anti-aircraft gun', 'fliegerabwehrkanone'.

Napoleon travelled to the battle of Waterloo in a lavishly upholstered bulletproof coach.

The first book ever printed in Gaelic was a translation of the Book of Common Prayer which appeared in 1567.

In spite of its name the Century plant blooms every seven or eight years.

Although you may feel warmer drinking alcohol your body temperature actually falls as a result of drinking it.

If called upon to swim, elephants can move through the water surprisingly well.

Shaving with an electric shaver in fact uses less energy than shaving with a hand razor and hot water.

The large ruby that is set in the Imperial State Crown, worn by English sovereigns on great occasions of state, was worn by Henry V at the battle of Agincourt in 1415 and was presented to the Black Prince by Pedro the Cruel of Castille in 1367.

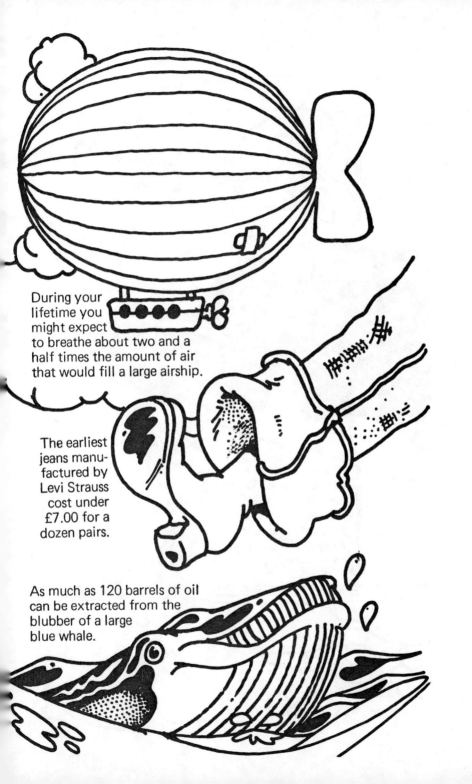

During your lifetime you might expect to breathe about two and a half times the amount of air that would fill a large airship.

The earliest jeans manufactured by Levi Strauss cost under £7.00 for a dozen pairs.

As much as 120 barrels of oil can be extracted from the blubber of a large blue whale.

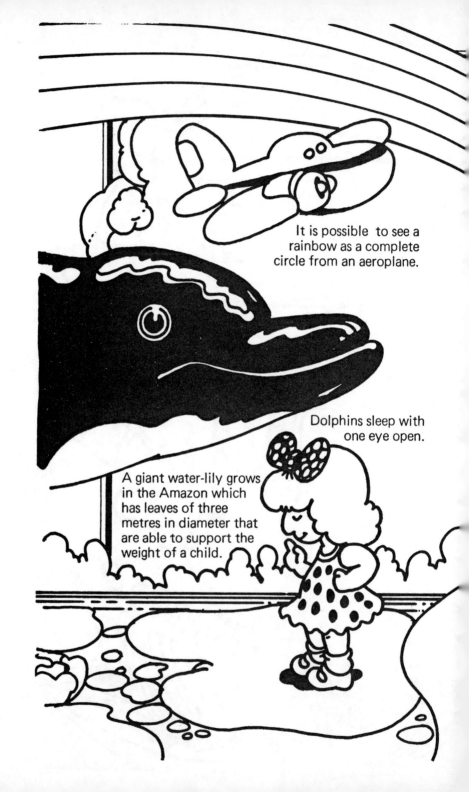

It is possible to see a rainbow as a complete circle from an aeroplane.

Dolphins sleep with one eye open.

A giant water-lily grows in the Amazon which has leaves of three metres in diameter that are able to support the weight of a child.

Nearly half the people on earth live in only one thirtieth of the total land area.

One fifth of the oxygen we inhale is used by the cells in the brain.

61

Peers of
the realm
can be
arrested for
felony and
treason, but
they cannot be
arrested for civil
offences.

During his expedition to
conquer Asia, Alexander
the Great instructed his
armourers to make pieces
of equipment, such as
helmets, several times
larger than those worn
by his troops. These were
then left for the enemy to
find in the hope that they
would become demora-
lised at the prospect of
fighting these conquering
'giants'.

At some stage in their varied careers Pope Pius XI, Mao Tse-Tung and Casanova were all librarians.

You can tell a fish's age by counting the rings on its scales in the same way that you can estimate the age of a tree by counting the rings in the trunk.

The sensation of weightlessness experienced on a journey to the moon was described by Bishop Francis Godwin in a book which was written in 1638.

At the age of ninety our hearts are pumping half the amount of blood they were pumping when we were twenty.

The London Brick Company can manufacture 17,000,000 bricks every week, an annual total of 884,000,000 bricks.

The total world catch of sea fish at the present represents slightly more than 5 per cent of the amount of edible food produced on land.

In China they not only eat soup made from birds' nests — they even prefer eggs that have been buried in the ground for three months while they 'ripen'.

Gambling dens in 18th century England employed one man with the sole responsibility of swallowing the dice if ever there was a raid.

Among the various new names suggested for the actress Marilyn Novak were: Iris Green, Kavin Novak and Windy City. These were discarded in favour of Kim Novak.

When Samuel Pepys was made secretary to the Navy Board in 1660, he knew nothing about the Navy and nothing about arithmetic, which was crucial to his job. Undeterred, he set about learning all he could, a process which included learning his multiplication tables at the age of thirty.

The prison on the Isle of Sark, in the Channel Islands, holds a maximum number of two prisoners.

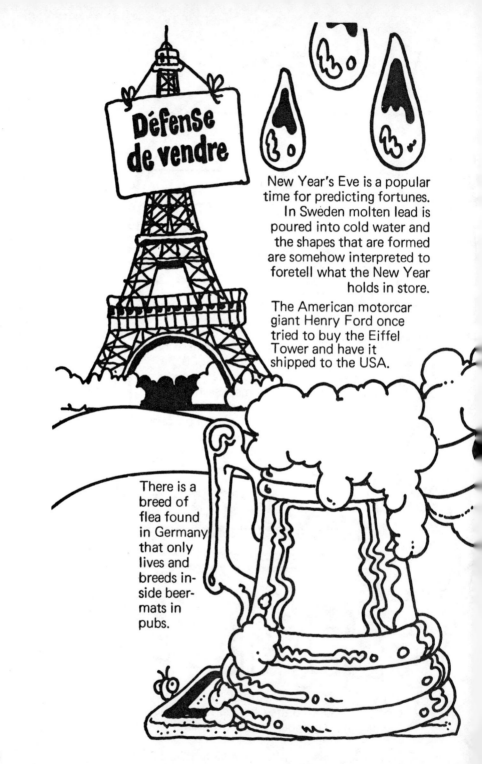

Défense de vendre

New Year's Eve is a popular time for predicting fortunes. In Sweden molten lead is poured into cold water and the shapes that are formed are somehow interpreted to foretell what the New Year holds in store.

The American motorcar giant Henry Ford once tried to buy the Eiffel Tower and have it shipped to the USA.

There is a breed of flea found in Germany that only lives and breeds inside beer-mats in pubs.

President Carter saw a UFO in 1969, during his birth month.

When Queen Victoria asked the Duke of Wellington how the sparrows could be persuaded to move from the trees that were to be enclosed by the Crystal Palace, the Iron Duke allegedly replied, 'Sparrowhawks, Ma'am'.

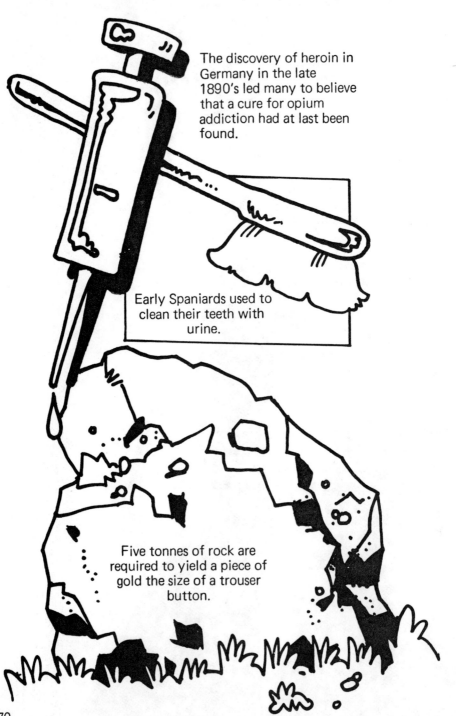

The discovery of heroin in Germany in the late 1890's led many to believe that a cure for opium addiction had at last been found.

Early Spaniards used to clean their teeth with urine.

Five tonnes of rock are required to yield a piece of gold the size of a trouser button.

Solid blocks of tea were used as currency in Siberia until the last century.

It has been estimated that the total number of people who died during the Black Death in the thirteenth century was equal to the present population of Turkey, over 42,000,000.

The Queen is forbidden to enter the House of Commons. The last monarch to do so was Charles I, and we all know what happened to him.

Following his victory at the battle of Hyderabad in 1843, the British commander Sir Charles Napier sent a despatch containing the single word 'peccavi'. It took the staff at headquarters some time to work out that it meant 'I have sinned' in Latin. Hyderabad is in the state of Sind.

Of the several species of shark swimming in the oceans less than ten have the teeth and jaws capable of eating a man and fewer than that have the desire to do so.

There are almost three times as many species of plants as there are of animals.

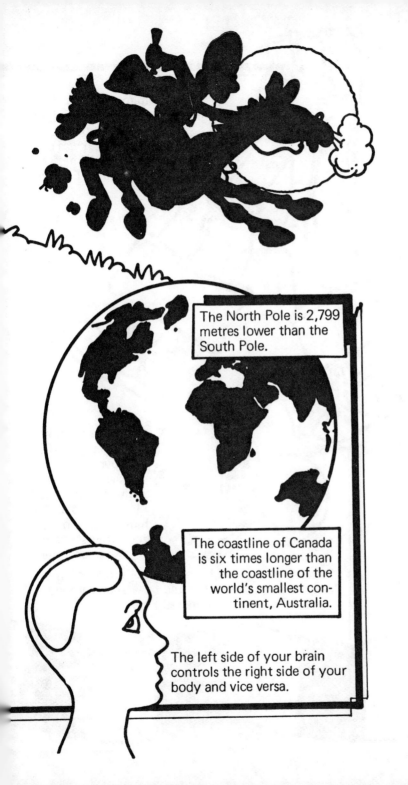

The North Pole is 2,799 metres lower than the South Pole.

The coastline of Canada is six times longer than the coastline of the world's smallest continent, Australia.

The left side of your brain controls the right side of your body and vice versa.

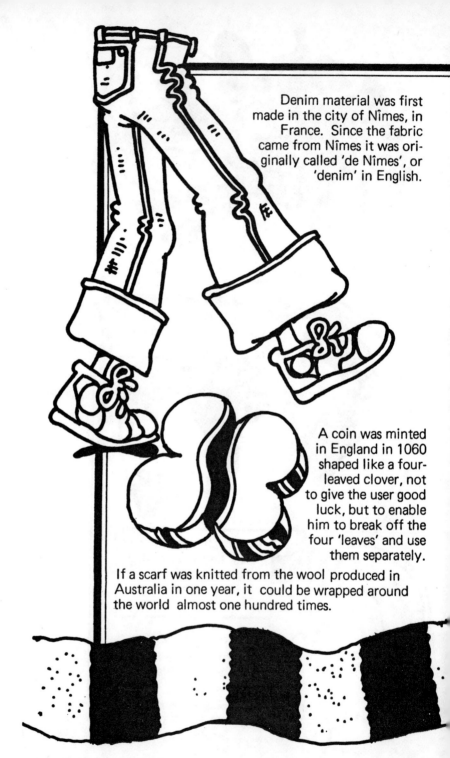

Denim material was first made in the city of Nîmes, in France. Since the fabric came from Nîmes it was originally called 'de Nîmes', or 'denim' in English.

A coin was minted in England in 1060 shaped like a four-leaved clover, not to give the user good luck, but to enable him to break off the four 'leaves' and use them separately.

If a scarf was knitted from the wool produced in Australia in one year, it could be wrapped around the world almost one hundred times.

Cow's milk can contain up to twice as much protein as human milk.

Although male seals are called bulls and female seals are called cows, their young are quite illogically called pups.

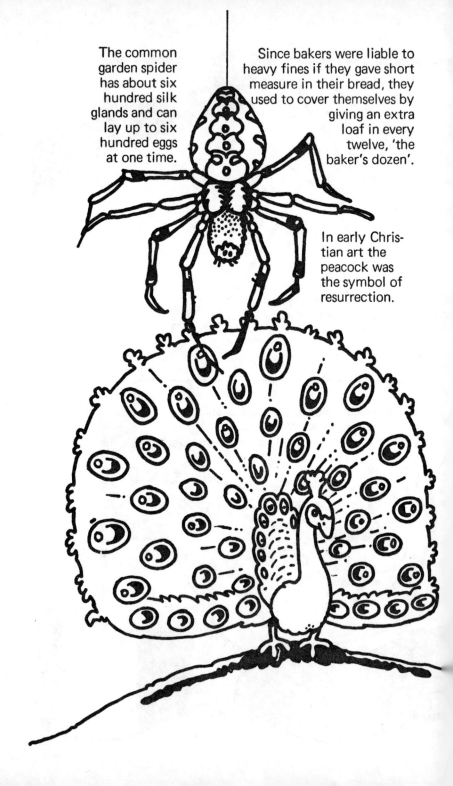

The common garden spider has about six hundred silk glands and can lay up to six hundred eggs at one time.

Since bakers were liable to heavy fines if they gave short measure in their bread, they used to cover themselves by giving an extra loaf in every twelve, 'the baker's dozen'.

In early Christian art the peacock was the symbol of resurrection.

Ismail the Blood-thirsty, sometime ruler of Morocco, is reputed to have fathered 548 sons and 340 daughters.

During the reign of George III, 6,500 tonnes of hair powder were used by the British Army every year.

As a young man Henry VIII was a celebrated hammer-thrower.

Before corks were fitted into wine bottles the Italians used to fill the necks with oil.

Half the world's wealth is owned by four countries whose total population is less than 15 per cent of the world's total.

The Colossus of Rhodes which was one of the grandest of the Seven Wonders of the Ancient World, was ignominiously carried off by the Arab invaders and the bronze that had covered it was sold for scrap.

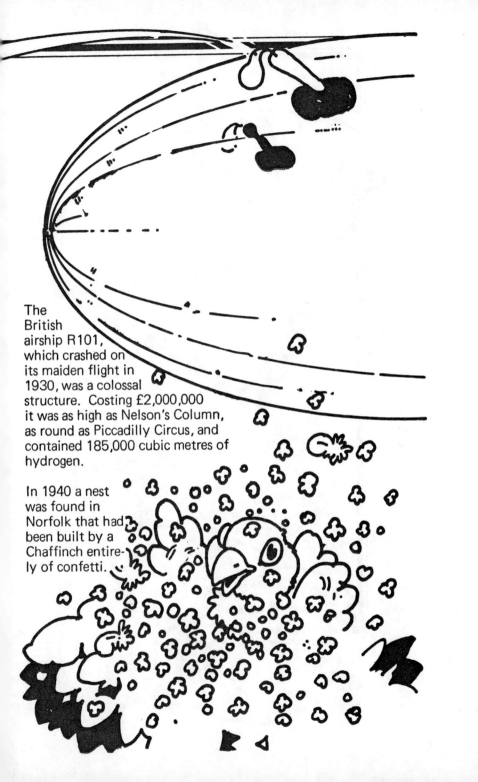

The British airship R101, which crashed on its maiden flight in 1930, was a colossal structure. Costing £2,000,000 it was as high as Nelson's Column, as round as Piccadilly Circus, and contained 185,000 cubic metres of hydrogen.

In 1940 a nest was found in Norfolk that had been built by a Chaffinch entirely of confetti.

The
elephant
is the only
animal that has
been taught to stand on its
head.

In the Middle Ages nearly
one day in three was a
religious holiday.

The complete root system
of the Pumpkin plant would
stretch for 24 kilometres, if
every root was laid end
to end.

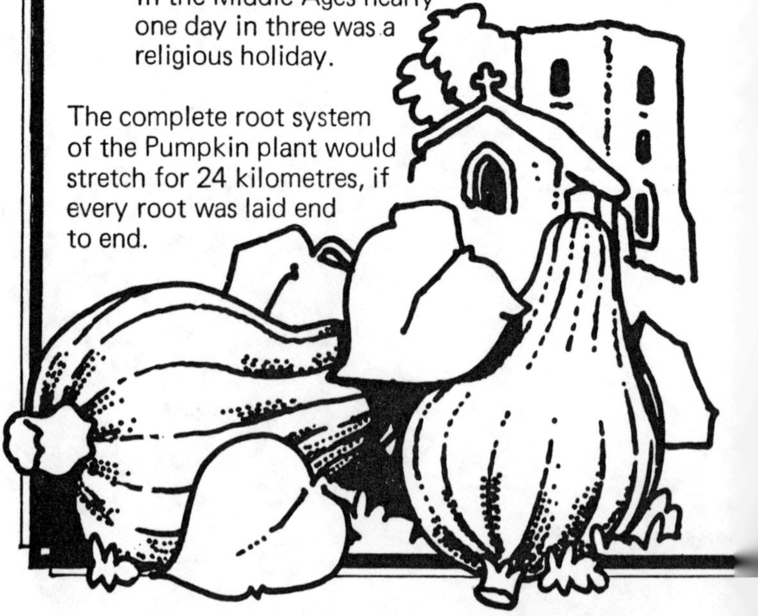

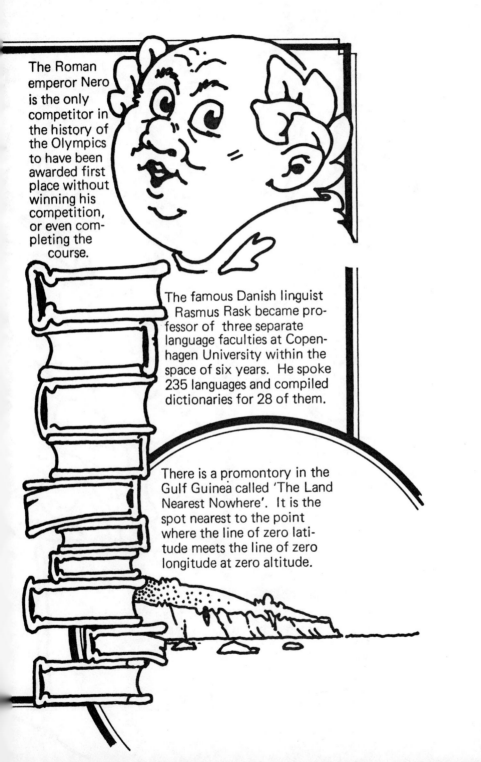

The Roman emperor Nero is the only competitor in the history of the Olympics to have been awarded first place without winning his competition, or even completing the course.

The famous Danish linguist Rasmus Rask became professor of three separate language faculties at Copenhagen University within the space of six years. He spoke 235 languages and compiled dictionaries for 28 of them.

There is a promontory in the Gulf Guinea called 'The Land Nearest Nowhere'. It is the spot nearest to the point where the line of zero latitude meets the line of zero longitude at zero altitude.

Pink elephants are not only products of alcoholic indulgence. In the Tsavo region of Kenya the elephants bathe in pink mud which dries on them when they leave the mud pools.

'Silk', 'tea' and 'tycoon' are all words that entered the English language from Chinese.

The world's most popular hobby is stamp collecting.

The first law passed against lynching in the USA made the accused liable to four years in prison.

Cleopatra's Needle, in London, has
no connection with that Egyptian
ruler except for the name. It was
erected in Egypt more than 1,400
years before Cleopatra's birth.

The first bikini appeared to the world
four days after the American atomic test
at Bikini Atoll in the Pacific. The creator
of the new costume, Louis Reard, chose the
name to express the idea of 'the ultimate'
and the model who wore the first bikini
reputedly received 50,000 fan letters.

An anagram of 'crinoline'
is 'inner coil'

Before driving licences were made Ernest Bond, of Bishopstone near Bristol, was riding around the countryside on a motor-cycle at the age of six.

The most recent type of Nissen hut was invented by the grandson of Peter Norman Nissen, who invented the bow-shaped hut roofed with corrugated iron. The modern hut is made of cardboard.

The Royal Mint
only produced
four pennies
in 1933.

Piano keys are generally made from the wood of the
Hornbeam.

Abraham Lincoln was the first US President to be assassinated.

The commonly used cheer, 'Hip, Hip, Hooray' is supposed to have originated from the conquest of Jerusalem by the Saracens.

During the bitterly cold winter of 1890-91 it was possible to skate the whole length of the frozen river Thames from Lechlade to Teddington, without interruption except for the locks.

Only the male canary sings.

Domestic cats spend only one third of their lives awake, compared with their owners who spend only one third of their lives asleep.

The redwood tree has fireproof bark.

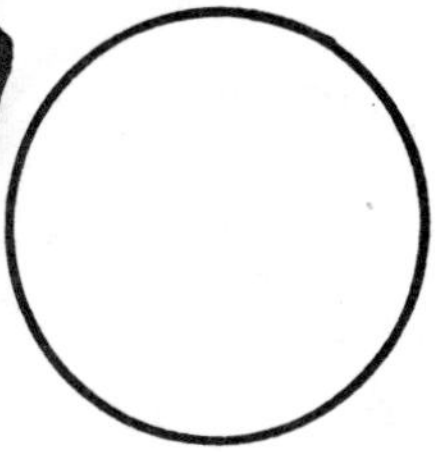

Saudi Arabia imports sand from Scotland and camels from North Africa.

Benjamin Hall, the eighteenth century politician, weighed 158 kilograms, which explains why the bell named after him is called Big Ben.

The Old Faithful geyser in the Yellowstone National Park, in the USA, shoots boiling water into the air every hour.

The worst tornado ever recorded hurtled over Texas at a speed only slightly slower than the official World Water Speed Record, 464.45 km/h.

Our muscles only work in one way, by pulling. They never push.

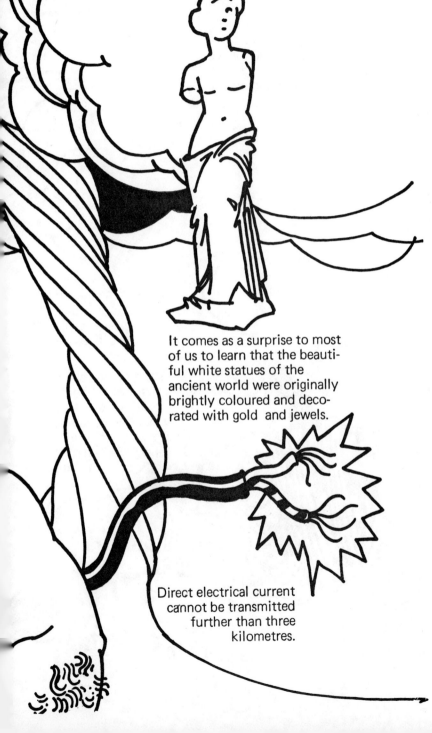

It comes as a surprise to most of us to learn that the beautiful white statues of the ancient world were originally brightly coloured and decorated with gold and jewels.

Direct electrical current cannot be transmitted further than three kilometres.

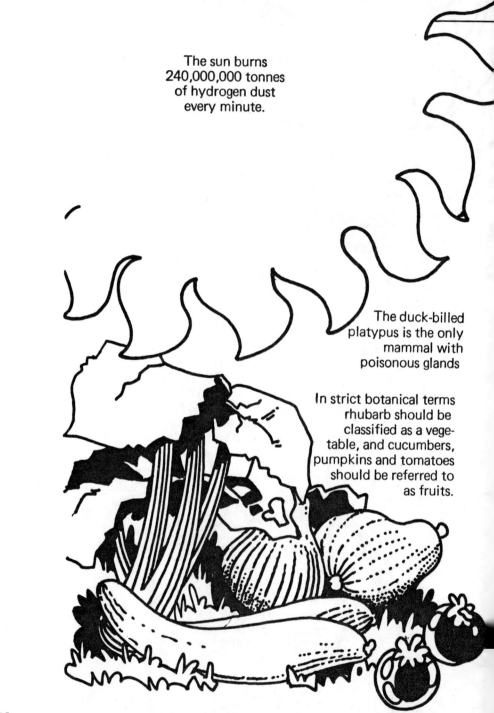

The sun burns
240,000,000 tonnes
of hydrogen dust
every minute.

The duck-billed
platypus is the only
mammal with
poisonous glands

In strict botanical terms
rhubarb should be
classified as a vege-
table, and cucumbers,
pumpkins and tomatoes
should be referred to
as fruits.

The first 'guinea-pigs' to undergo smallpox vaccination in England were seven eighteenth century criminals. As a reward they were pardoned — after their recovery.

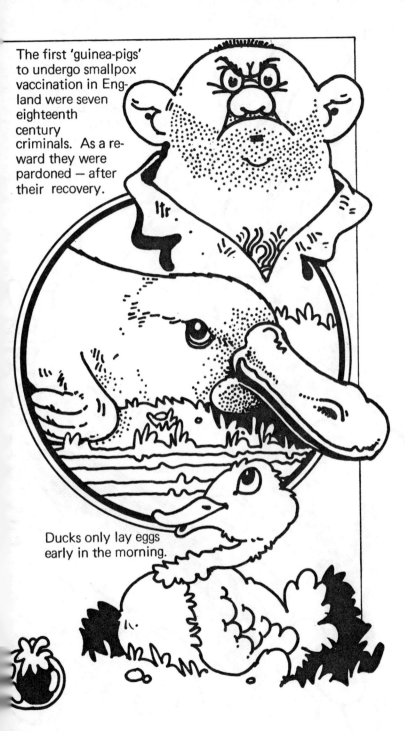

Ducks only lay eggs early in the morning.

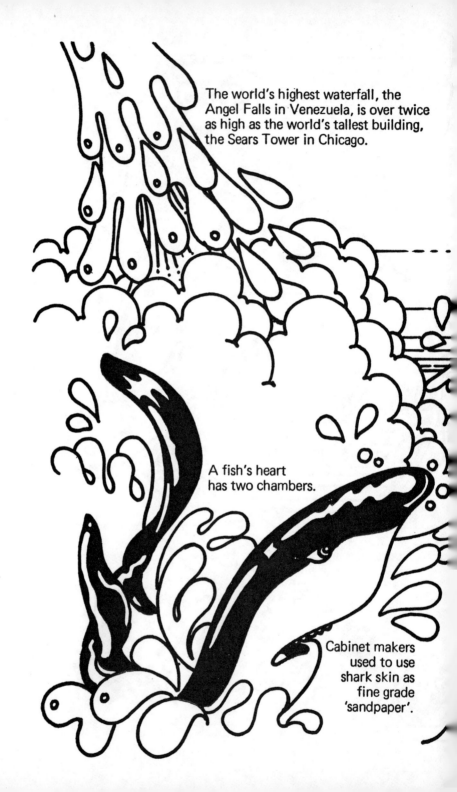

The world's highest waterfall, the Angel Falls in Venezuela, is over twice as high as the world's tallest building, the Sears Tower in Chicago.

A fish's heart has two chambers.

Cabinet makers used to use shark skin as fine grade 'sandpaper'.

Man is too heavy and his body is the wrong shape to be able to fly like a bird under his own power. A man weighing 68 kg would require a breastbone two metres long to hold all the muscles for powering a pair of wings that could lift him off the ground.

The sun weighs 330,000 times as much as the earth.

If you travel due north from Belem, near the mouth of the Amazon in Brazil, you will not reach land until you arrive on the coast of Greenland.

During the sixteenth century no Japanese was allowed to leave Japan without official permission. Breaking this law resulted in immediate execution.

The rotation of the earth causes any given point on the equator to travel at an average speed of 29 kilometres per minute.

Picking mushrooms is protected by law in Sweden — everyone is allowed access to the forests where they grow.

Workers in oil fields
in the Sahara are each
allocated 7.5 litres of
water per day for drin-
king and cooking alone.

Bungalows are named after the
Hindi word 'bangla' which
means 'belonging to Bengal'.

Flies generally prefer to breed in the centre of a room.

According to ancient Moslem tradition Eve ate a fig in the garden of Eden, not an apple. In fact there is no reference in the Bible to an apple either.

The sailfish can swim faster than a horse can gallop.

If a hole was dug straight through the earth from Shanghai, it would come out on the other side of the globe very near Buenos Aires.

In India the Chenchu tribe believe that sex at night produces blind children.

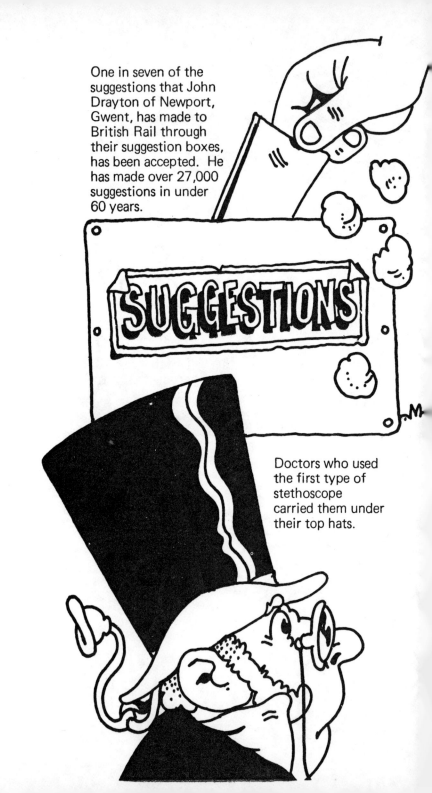

One in seven of the suggestions that John Drayton of Newport, Gwent, has made to British Rail through their suggestion boxes, has been accepted. He has made over 27,000 suggestions in under 60 years.

Doctors who used the first type of stethoscope carried them under their top hats.

Ostrich races are held in South Africa with jockeys mounted on saddles on the birds' backs.

Only two types of mice are found in Ireland.

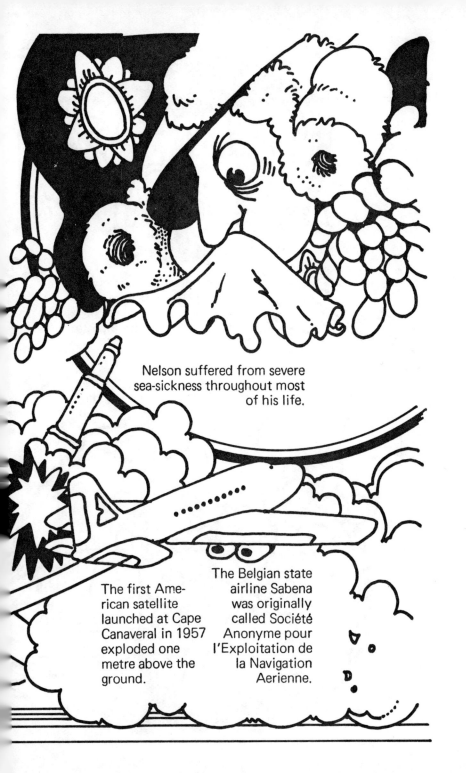

Nelson suffered from severe sea-sickness throughout most of his life.

The first American satellite launched at Cape Canaveral in 1957 exploded one metre above the ground.

The Belgian state airline Sabena was originally called Société Anonyme pour l'Exploitation de la Navigation Aerienne.

Brushing your teeth with salt cleans them as effectively as brushing them with toothpaste.

Horses can fall asleep standing up.

It would take 27,000,000,000 balls the size of our sun to make one the size of the enormous red star called Epsilon Aurigae.

A belief is widely held in certain areas of France that if a bachelor steps on a cat's tail he will not find a wife for at least another year.

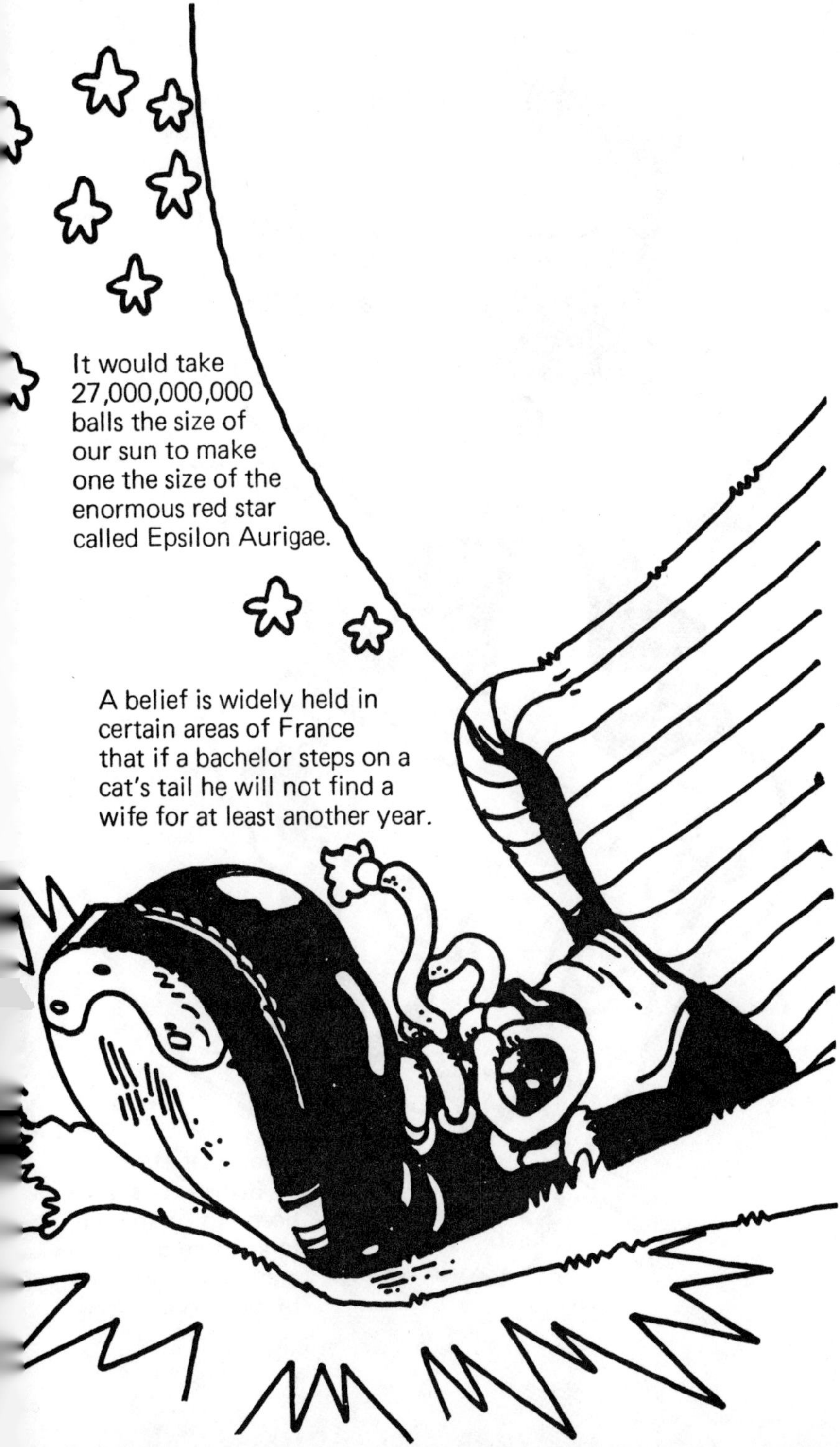

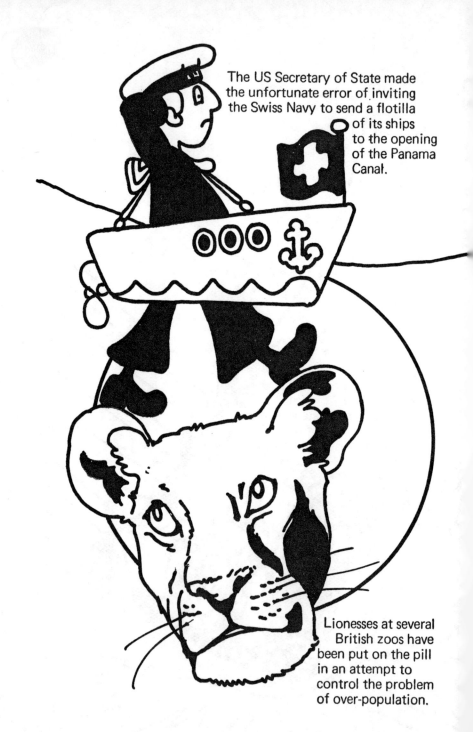

The US Secretary of State made the unfortunate error of inviting the Swiss Navy to send a flotilla of its ships to the opening of the Panama Canal.

Lionesses at several British zoos have been put on the pill in an attempt to control the problem of over-population.

Food experts do not share the enthusiasm of the Lapps for reindeer meat. According to the experts the only part of the reindeer worth eating is its tongue, and even that has to be smoked first.

The song 'Half a Pound of Tuppenny Rice, Half a Pound of Treacle' is bitter comment on inflation and the rising cost of living. The phrase 'Pop goes the weasel' refers to the desperate situation of pawning ('pop') the tools of one's trade ('weasel') in order to buy the next meal.

Before the dawn of modern medical practice bone-setting was the province of the blacksmith in England.

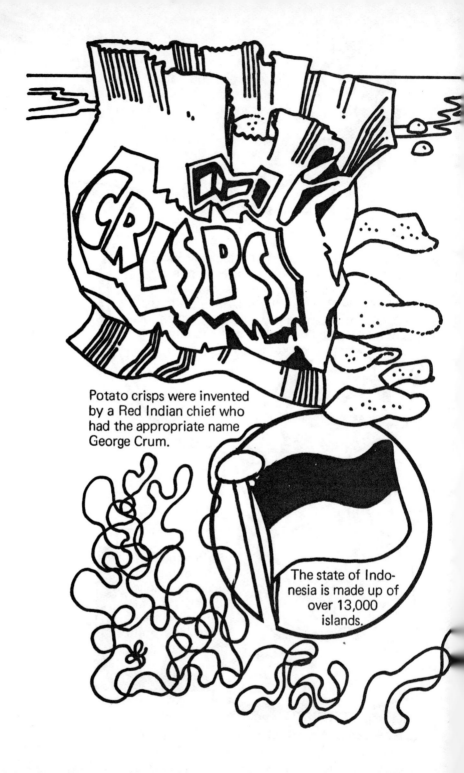

Potato crisps were invented by a Red Indian chief who had the appropriate name George Crum.

The state of Indonesia is made up of over 13,000 islands.

In Cuba there is an unusual farm with very unusual stock. The enterprising farmer breeds crocodiles; there are normally about 12,000 on the farm at any one time.

In 1975 an American was arrested after trying to drown his wife in a waterbed.

Originally a 'clue' was a ball of thread or wool, which explains the metaphor of 'unravelling' the clues of a mystery.

109

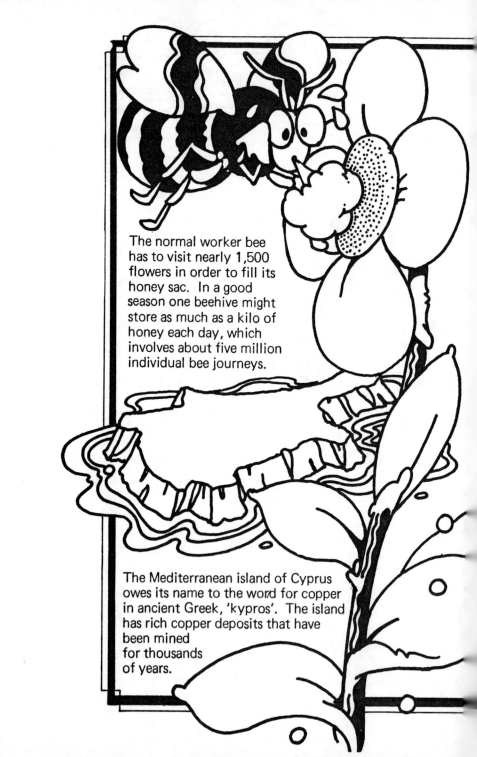

The normal worker bee has to visit nearly 1,500 flowers in order to fill its honey sac. In a good season one beehive might store as much as a kilo of honey each day, which involves about five million individual bee journeys.

The Mediterranean island of Cyprus owes its name to the word for copper in ancient Greek, 'kypros'. The island has rich copper deposits that have been mined for thousands of years.

When Eskimos buy refrigerators they often use them to stop their food from freezing.

It takes 40 years for vintage port to reach its ideal state of maturity.

A law in the mid west state of Indiana, USA, prohibits you from travelling on a bus within four hours of eating garlic.

The Dead Sea is so salty that it is impossible to drown in it unless you are held under water.

There are more lakes in Canada than in the rest of the world put together.

The human brain uses the same amount of power as a ten-watt electric bulb.

If they are near water raccoons often wash their food before they eat it.

Seaweed is used in the manufacture of a wide variety of products, including fertilisers, medicines, paint, toothpaste and even ice-cream.

The cantilever brassière was the brainchild of the eccentric millionaire Howard Hughes.

1858 was the year of the Great Stink of London. The combination of an unusually low rainfall with a very hot summer caused the river Thames to reek appallingly and the windows of the House of Commons were hung with curtains drenched in chloride of lime to counteract the smell.

Dieting was principally a male preoccupation until after the First World War, when female fashion disposed of corsets and stays and excess flesh became more evident.

The two largest cities in the Netherlands, Amsterdam and Rotterdam, and half the area of the country, lie below sea level.

A study conducted into colds revealed that people were more likely to catch colds when their mothers-in-law came to stay.

The Icelandic parliament, the Althing, was established in 930 and it has been governing the country for over 1,000 years since then.

Although Switzerland never goes to war, military training is compulsory and 350,000 troops can be mobilised in a single day.

117

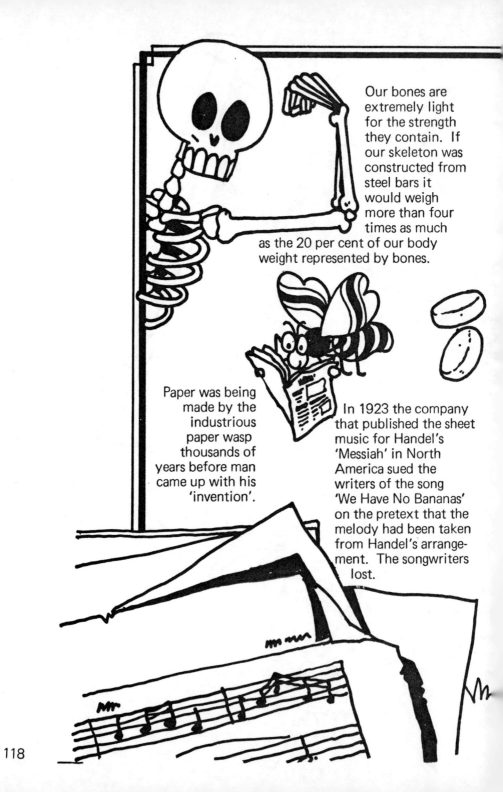

Our bones are extremely light for the strength they contain. If our skeleton was constructed from steel bars it would weigh more than four times as much as the 20 per cent of our body weight represented by bones.

Paper was being made by the industrious paper wasp thousands of years before man came up with his 'invention'.

In 1923 the company that published the sheet music for Handel's 'Messiah' in North America sued the writers of the song 'We Have No Bananas' on the pretext that the melody had been taken from Handel's arrangement. The songwriters lost.

The tranquilliser Valium is the most widely used drug on earth.

Medieval German men used to go to the barber to have a bath as well as a haircut.

Surveys have shown that only one per cent of the male population of France have enough stamina after the week-end to make love on Monday.

Virtually all the fish in the world are caught in waters over the continental shelves, which make up less than 10 per cent of the area of the oceans.

Queen Victoria never permitted the Royal
Train to travel faster than 30 miles an hour.
On one occasion when she found out that
it had touched 40 miles an hour, she ordered
the driver to be whipped and dismissed.

The Russo-Japanese
War of 1904-05 was
perhaps the first war
in history in which
more casualties arose
from wounds than
from disease.

Lord's cricket ground was originally in Dorset Square.

Nearly half the heat which your body loses is lost through the top of your head.

By observing which leg a man puts into his trousers first, you can usually tell whether he is left-handed or right-handed.

Nothing female is allowed on to the peninsula of Mount Athos in northern Greece, which is inhabited exclusively by monks.

A certain George Thornton was fined for speeding in Cardiff in 1901. He had been driving at 10 miles an hour.

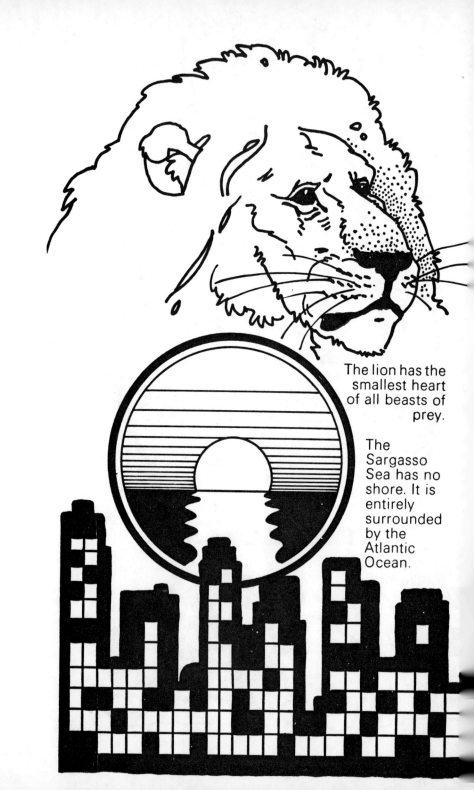

The lion has the smallest heart of all beasts of prey.

The Sargasso Sea has no shore. It is entirely surrounded by the Atlantic Ocean.

Every corpse in New Orleans has to be buried in a mausoleum because the ground is too damp for normal interment.

The Turks call a turkey an 'American bird'

In August 1972 the murder rate in New York was running at thirteen a day.

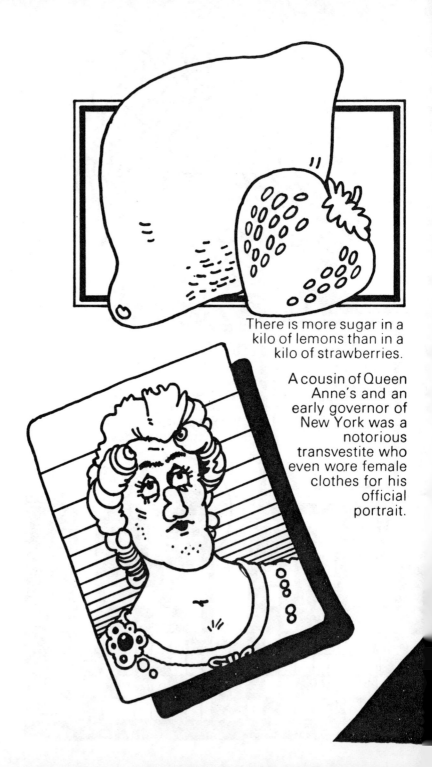

There is more sugar in a kilo of lemons than in a kilo of strawberries.

A cousin of Queen Anne's and an early governor of New York was a notorious transvestite who even wore female clothes for his official portrait.

The greatest British playwright who ever wrote for the stage, William Shakespeare, never saw an actress in his life.

Garlic belongs to the Lily family.

The sign of the cross in China used to indicate a pawn-shop.

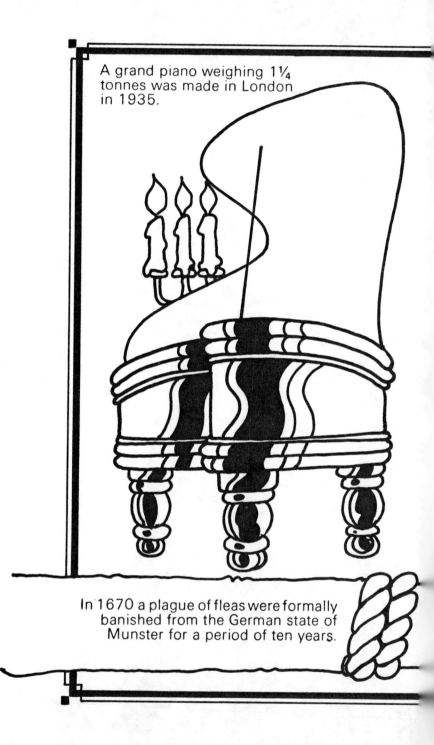

A grand piano weighing 1¼ tonnes was made in London in 1935.

In 1670 a plague of fleas were formally banished from the German state of Munster for a period of ten years.

The expression of referring to someone as a 'brick' was first recorded by Plutarch who quoted a Spartan statesman Aesilas, who referred to the Spartan army as the bricks which made the state powerful and enduring.

King Alphonse of Spain was actually born a king and he received the oath of fidelity when he was only one month old.

Cyanide poisoning can be produced from the stones of plums, apricots and cherries, as well as from apple pips.

Half a mile from the site of an atomic explosion the blast still travels at over 1,200 km/h.

St. Patrick's Cathedral in Dublin is a Protestant church.

The so-called four elements, earth, air, fire and water are not elements at all but compounds.

The Weihenstephen Brewery in Bavaria has been brewing beer for over 900 years. It had been in business for twenty-six years when William the Conqueror defeated King Harold at Hastings.

The largest shadow that we are ever likely to see is the one cast by the earth on the surface of the moon during an eclipse.

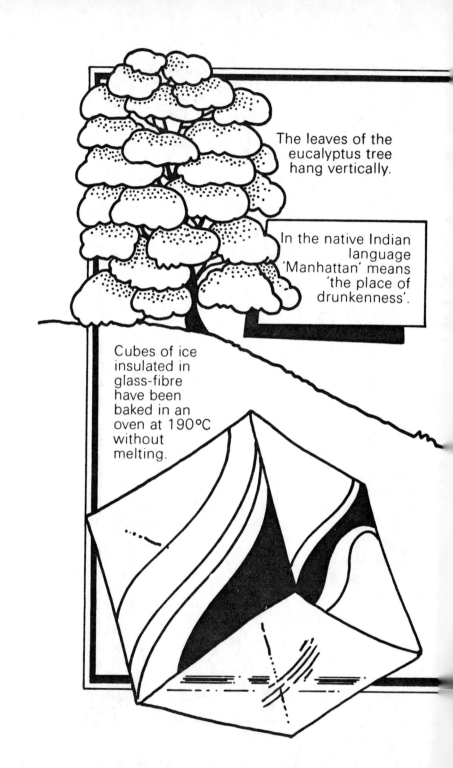

The leaves of the eucalyptus tree hang vertically.

In the native Indian language 'Manhattan' means 'the place of drunkenness'.

Cubes of ice insulated in glass-fibre have been baked in an oven at 190°C without melting.

Homer and Socrates are considered to be two of the greatest figures of literary history, although nothing they actually wrote has survived.

There is no such thing as one dice. Strictly speaking the singular form of dice is 'die'.

The frog's tongue grows from the front of its mouth which makes it easier for it to catch insects.

The cracking sound made by a whip is caused by the tip moving faster than the speed of sound.

Submarines can only lie still on the bottom, at other depths they must either keep moving or rise to the surface.

The method of execution in Mongolia practised until comparatively recently consisted of nailing the condemned prisoner into a wooden box and then leaving him on the steppe.

In good agricultural conditions cereals produce double the amount of calories produced by dairy farming.

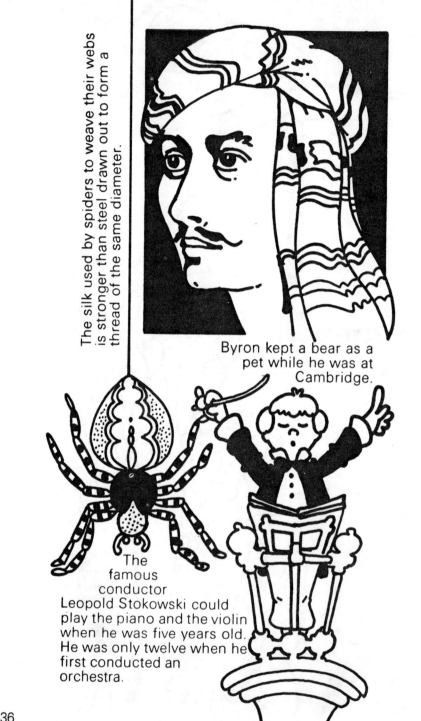

The silk used by spiders to weave their webs is stronger than steel drawn out to form a thread of the same diameter.

Byron kept a bear as a pet while he was at Cambridge.

The famous conductor Leopold Stokowski could play the piano and the violin when he was five years old. He was only twelve when he first conducted an orchestra.

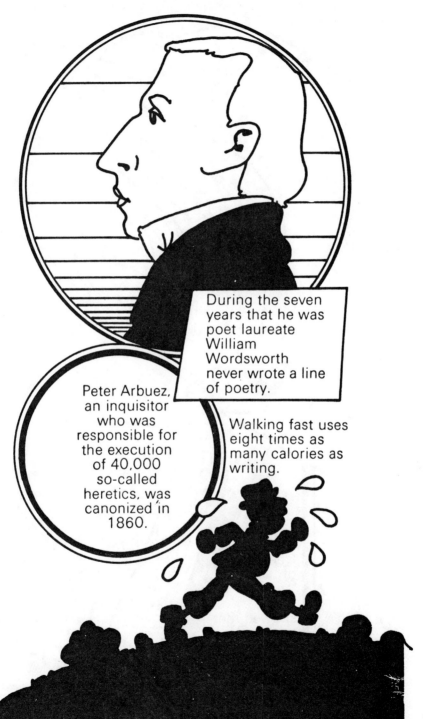

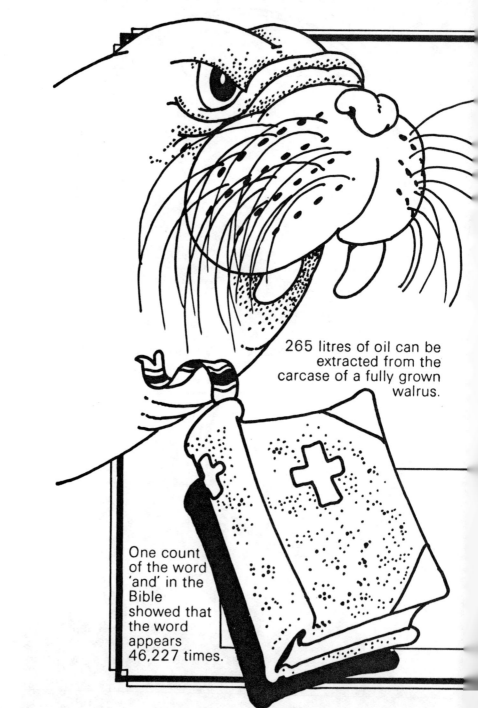

265 litres of oil can be extracted from the carcase of a fully grown walrus.

One count of the word 'and' in the Bible showed that the word appears 46,227 times.

A shark's skeleton is made of cartilage, it has no bone.

It is possible to bore holes in solid material with a noise of 210 decibels.

Louise Elizabeth Vaughan is probably only rivalled by the Virgin Mary as a mother in religious circles. She gave birth to one cardinal, two bishops, three priests and five nuns.

The American composer John Cage composed a piece of music entitled '4 minutes 33 seconds' which is totally silent.

While he was Prince Regent, George IV used to maintain a pale, elegant appearance by being frequently bled.

Lead and tin melt at 326.6° and 230°C respectively.

However, solder which is formed by combining the two metals, melts at 180°C.

The German statesman and linguist Karl Wilhelm von Humboldt composed a one hundred line poem in honour of his wife every day for forty days.

More than a third of the world's commercial supply of pineapples are grown in Hawaii.

The leaves on holly trees become less prickly the higher they grow on the tree.

American Indians used to smoke through their noses. They had special pipes that fitted into their nostrils.

The Mona Lisa was first bought by Francis I, King of France, who used it to decorate his bathroom.

There is a town called Å in Sweden.

The liver of a basking shark can represent as much as 10 per cent of its body weight.

The Ashmolean
Museum in Oxford is
the oldest museum in
the world. It dates from
1679.

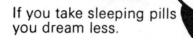

If you take sleeping pills
you dream less.

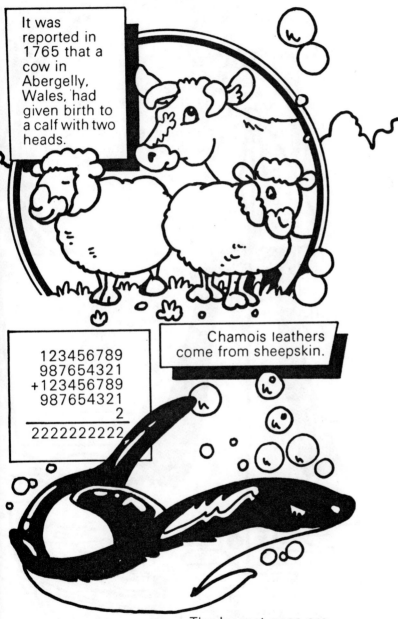

It was reported in 1765 that a cow in Abergelly, Wales, had given birth to a calf with two heads.

Chamois leathers come from sheepskin.

```
  123456789
  987654321
+ 123456789
  987654321
          2
───────────
2222222222
```

The largest eggs are laid by sharks.

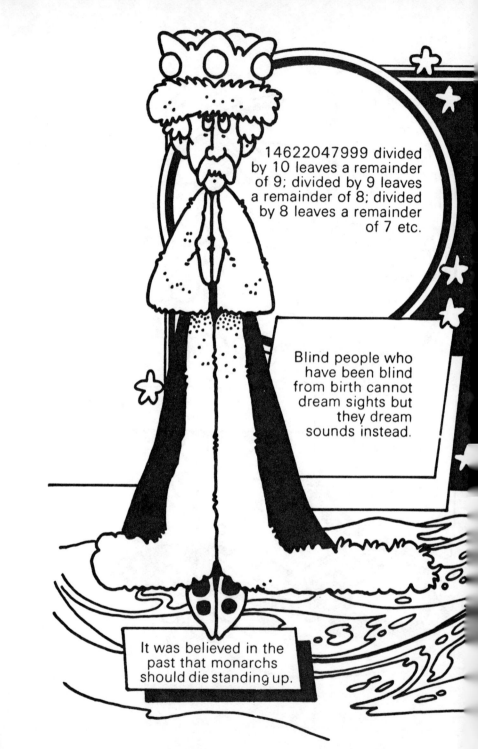

14622047999 divided by 10 leaves a remainder of 9; divided by 9 leaves a remainder of 8; divided by 8 leaves a remainder of 7 etc.

Blind people who have been blind from birth cannot dream sights but they dream sounds instead.

It was believed in the past that monarchs should die standing up.

One of the two moons that orbits the planet Neptune is so erratic that it varies between 1,610,000 km and 9,655,000 km from the planet's surface.

The nets drawn by large trawlers are each longer than a football pitch.

Falling from an altitude of 6,100 metres Harold Parkhurst shaved himself and lit a cigarette in mid-air before opening his parachute.

A dwarf at the court of King Charles II, called Geoffry Hudson, once fought a duel against a man twice his height and won. The cause of the duel was a woman, and Hudson won her also.

The Canadian river flows nowhere near Canada.

No matter how low the temperature falls outside, the windows of an empty house never frost over.

The anatomy department of Oxford University was deprived of one of its recently acquired corpses in December 1650. The body of Anne Greene was still living after being hanged for murder and the 'deceased' was revived and made a complete recovery.

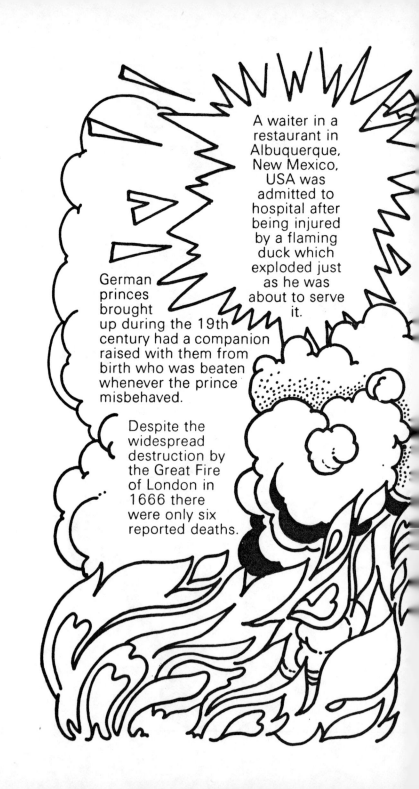

A waiter in a restaurant in Albuquerque, New Mexico, USA was admitted to hospital after being injured by a flaming duck which exploded just as he was about to serve it.

German princes brought up during the 19th century had a companion raised with them from birth who was beaten whenever the prince misbehaved.

Despite the widespread destruction by the Great Fire of London in 1666 there were only six reported deaths.

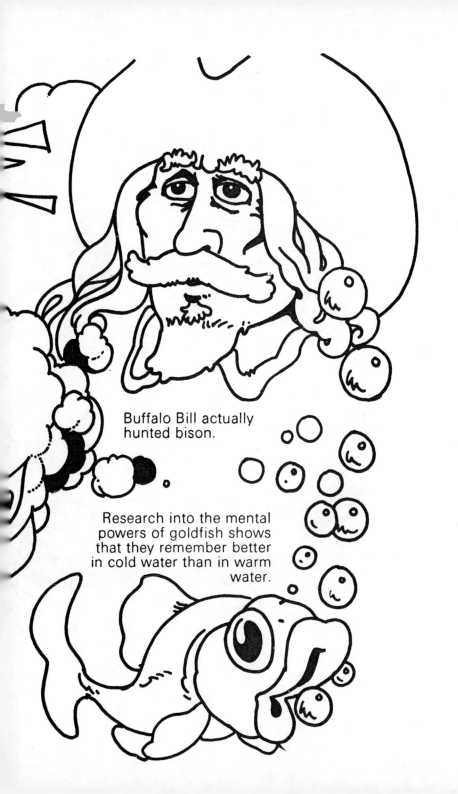

Buffalo Bill actually hunted bison.

Research into the mental powers of goldfish shows that they remember better in cold water than in warm water.

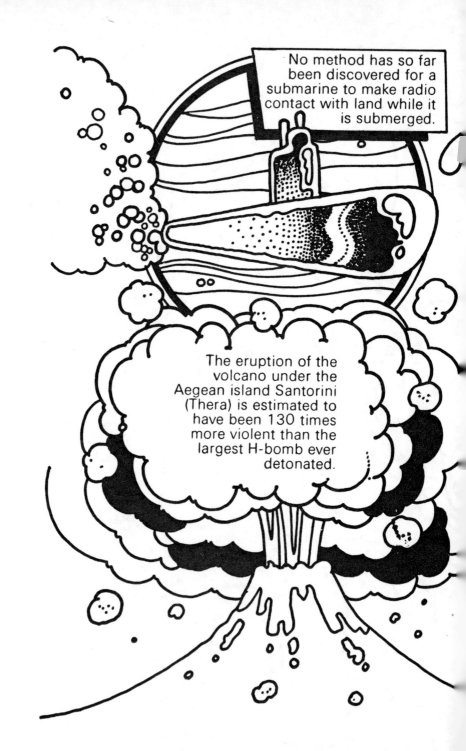

Plasma is 91 per cent water.

In the jargon of the oil industry a 'dry hole' refers to a well filled with water.

William the Conqueror is said to have been able to fire an arrow while sitting in a saddle from a bow which most men were unable to draw when they were standing upright on the ground.

A mature beech tree may give off as much as 680 litres of water on a warm, windy day.

Marble Arch in London was originally built as the main entrance to Buckingham Palace. After it had been built it was discovered that it was too narrow to allow a stage-coach to pass through.

Walter Watts crossed Canada from Vancouver to Halifax in 93 days, covering the 7,322 km journey on a unicycle.

The amount of water frozen in the Antarctic ice-cap is roughly equal to about 9 per cent of the contents of the Atlantic Ocean.

There are three thousand islands in the Caribbean Bahama chain and only twenty of these are inhabited.

Camels were being used in the Arizonan deserts as recently as 1870.

The founder of the Persian Empire, Cyrus the Great, once sentenced a river to death after one of his most valued horses had been drowned while crossing it. The river was actually made to disappear for more than 1,000 years.

The Matani tribe that used to inhabit part of West Africa played football with an unusual ball. They used a human skull.

The legendary medieval Spanish warrior called El Cid led his army to battle against the Moors after his death.

Miss Fanny Miles of Cincinnati, Ohio, U.S.A. had feet that were 60 cms long.

Pythagoras invented a club whose members were not allowed to eat beans or poke fires with iron objects.

The Douglas fir is a type of pine tree.

Sound travels so well in the Arctic that on a still day it is possible to hear an ordinary conversation from a distance of three kilometres.

159

When he was only twelve years old Robert, later Lord, Clive organised a protection racket in his home town of Market Drayton.

Koala bears get their name from the aboriginal words which mean 'no drink'.

Bombay duck is
made from dried
fish and curry.

Japanese saké is
correctly drunk from
little bowls or cups that
emit a whistling sound
when you drink from them.

A widely held
belief among
anthropologists
is that early
man was
singing long
before he was
able to
communicate
by the
spoken word.

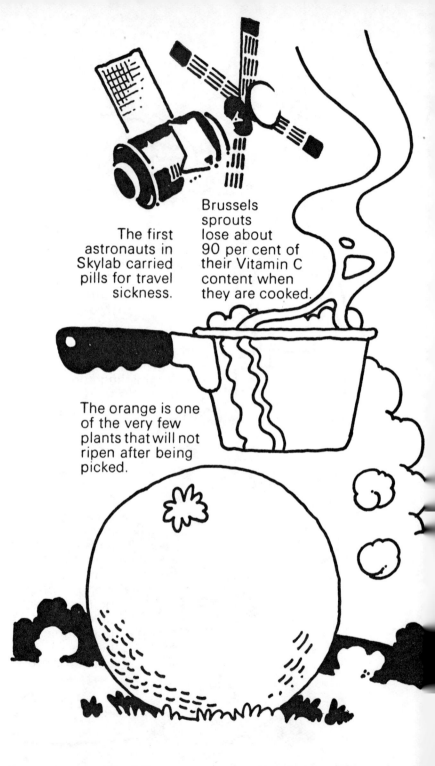

The first astronauts in Skylab carried pills for travel sickness.

Brussels sprouts lose about 90 per cent of their Vitamin C content when they are cooked.

The orange is one of the very few plants that will not ripen after being picked.

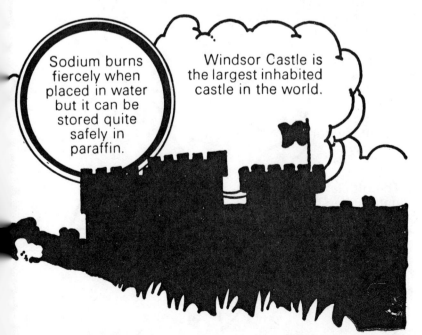

The employee at the Louvre
who stole the Mona Lisa, the
world's most famous painting, hid it for two
years and then tried to sell it for almost £50,000,
received a sentence of only one year fifteen days
for his crime. He convinced the court in his native
Italy that his motives were simply patriotic, he
wanted the painting to return to its homeland.

Sodium burns
fiercely when
placed in water
but it can be
stored quite
safely in
paraffin.

Windsor Castle is
the largest inhabited
castle in the world.

X-rays were first identified by a German physicist called Wilhelm Röntgen. The first X-ray was probably of his wife's hand, when she accidentally got in the way.

The official national emblem of Wales is a daffodil, not a leek.

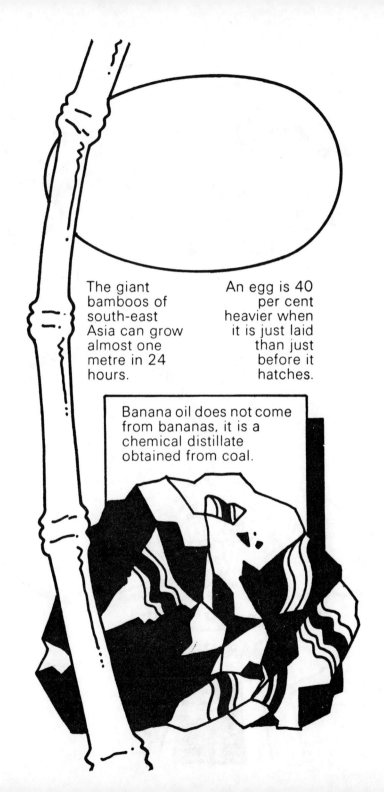

The giant bamboos of south-east Asia can grow almost one metre in 24 hours.

An egg is 40 per cent heavier when it is just laid than just before it hatches.

Banana oil does not come from bananas, it is a chemical distillate obtained from coal.

Gunpowder was first used by British forces at the battle of Crecy in 1346, one hundred years after the Chinese troops had used it against the invading Mongols.

A tenth century governor of Shansi province in China called Liu Ch'ung had four pupils in his eyes, two in each.

Byron learnt Cockney slang from an Italian cardinal who had never left Italy in his life.

BARNET

There
are always
slight flaws
in Persian carpets
since the Moslem creed
holds that perfection in
anything human is an offence
to Allah.

Only fifty kilometres
beneath the earth's
surface the
temperature
reaches the
melting
point of
rocks.

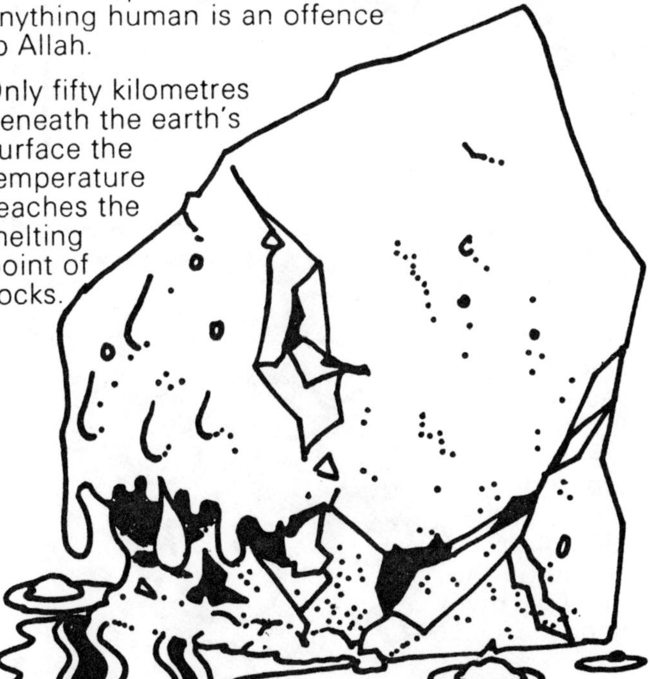

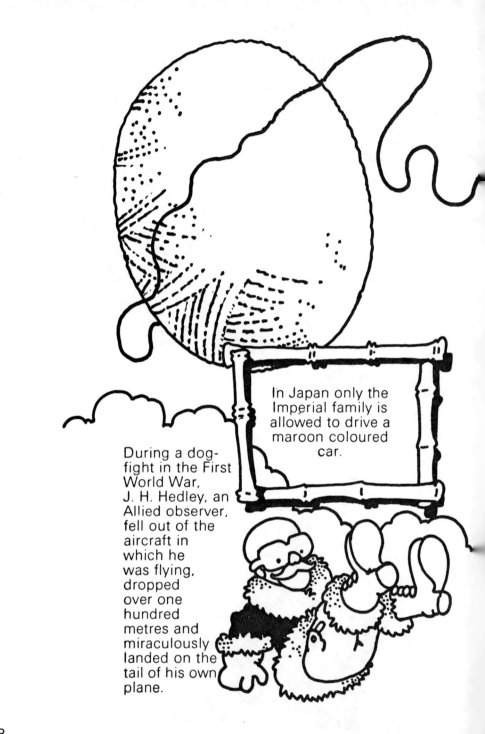

In Japan only the Imperial family is allowed to drive a maroon coloured car.

During a dog-fight in the First World War, J. H. Hedley, an Allied observer, fell out of the aircraft in which he was flying, dropped over one hundred metres and miraculously landed on the tail of his own plane.

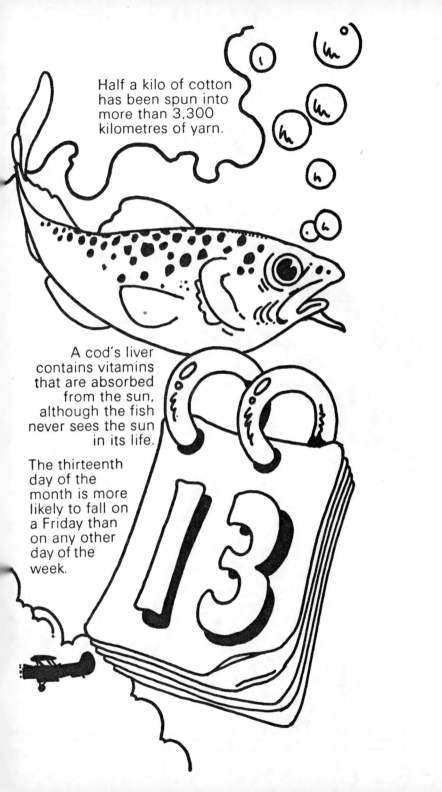

Half a kilo of cotton has been spun into more than 3,300 kilometres of yarn.

A cod's liver contains vitamins that are absorbed from the sun, although the fish never sees the sun in its life.

The thirteenth day of the month is more likely to fall on a Friday than on any other day of the week.

The hair spring of a
watch was originally
a pig's hair.

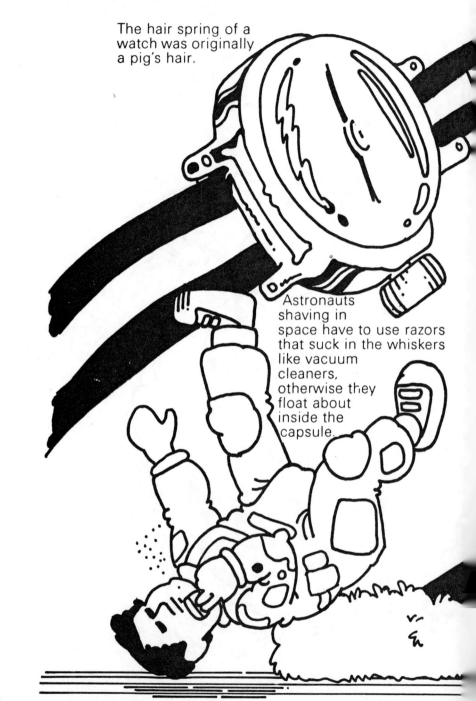

Astronauts
shaving in
space have to use razors
that suck in the whiskers
like vacuum
cleaners,
otherwise they
float about
inside the
capsule.

In France A.M. is in fact
P.M. Après-midi means
afternoon.

The coronation robe
worn by Emperor
Bokassa of the
Central African
Empire at his
coronation
cost over
£77,000 in
1977. His
country is
one of the
poorest
in
Africa.

A cat's eyes glow at night because they have a layer of cells in the inner eye that reflect light.

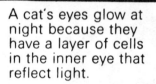

Termites can produce substances in their bodies that can rust metal, disintegrate glass and burn through lead.

It would take three and a half minutes to receive a radio message sent from Mars.

There are seventeen times as many calories in 100 g of raw celery as there are in the same amount of coffee.

The only way that Columbus ever signed his name was Cristobal Colon.

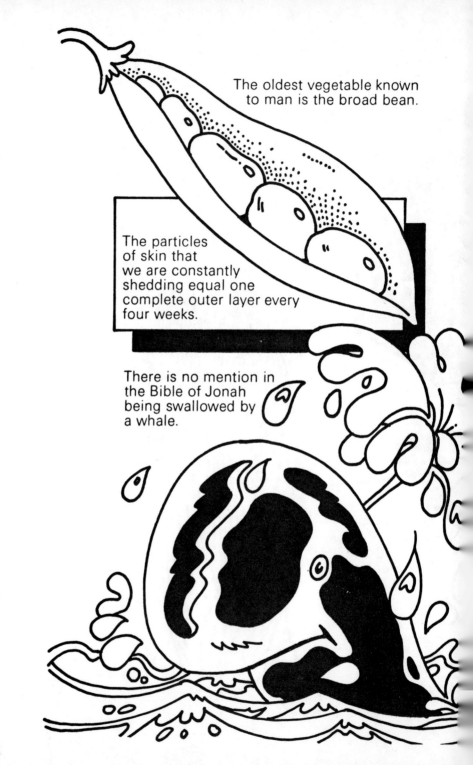

The oldest vegetable known to man is the broad bean.

The particles of skin that we are constantly shedding equal one complete outer layer every four weeks.

There is no mention in the Bible of Jonah being swallowed by a whale.

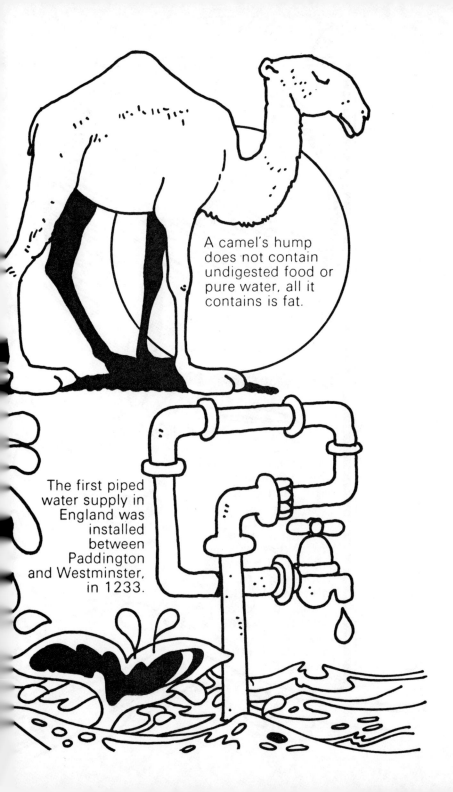

A camel's hump does not contain undigested food or pure water, all it contains is fat.

The first piped water supply in England was installed between Paddington and Westminster, in 1233.

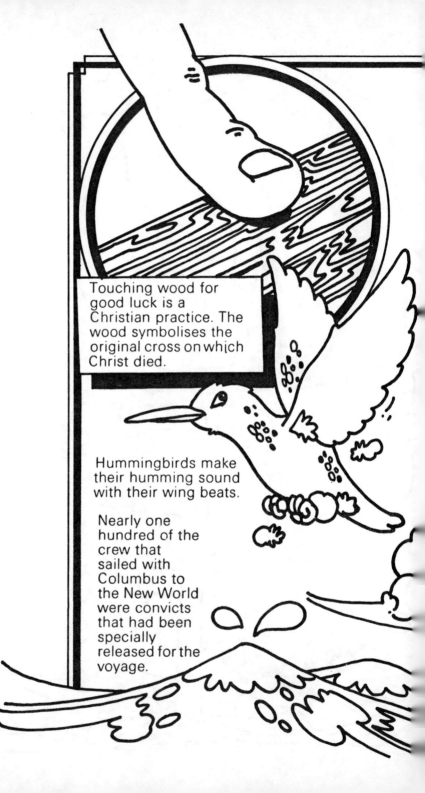

Touching wood for good luck is a Christian practice. The wood symbolises the original cross on which Christ died.

Hummingbirds make their humming sound with their wing beats.

Nearly one hundred of the crew that sailed with Columbus to the New World were convicts that had been specially released for the voyage.

Not only was Cleopatra the product of a brother and sister marriage, she married two of her own brothers as well.

At first tomatoes were only grown as decorative garden plants because they were considered to be poisonous.

Ladies with double chins used to be hoisted into the air by a strap beneath their jaw as part of their 'beauty treatment' in early English beauty parlours.

Rice paper is made from pitch or wood-pulp not from rice.

Pirates used to wear earrings because they believed that they improved their eyesight. Other people believe that earrings can relieve sore eyes and the Chinese insert acupuncture needles into the same point in the ear lobe to control senses in the eye.

The artist Edward Dickinson once won second prize in an American national art competition for a work which had been exhibited and judged hanging upside down.

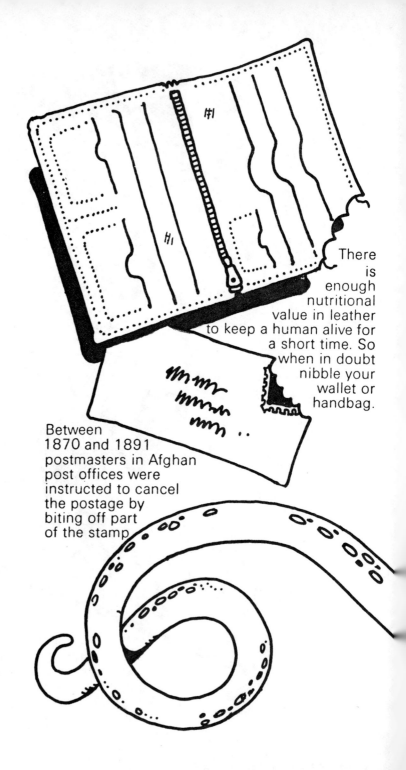

There is enough nutritional value in leather to keep a human alive for a short time. So when in doubt nibble your wallet or handbag.

Between 1870 and 1891 postmasters in Afghan post offices were instructed to cancel the postage by biting off part of the stamp.

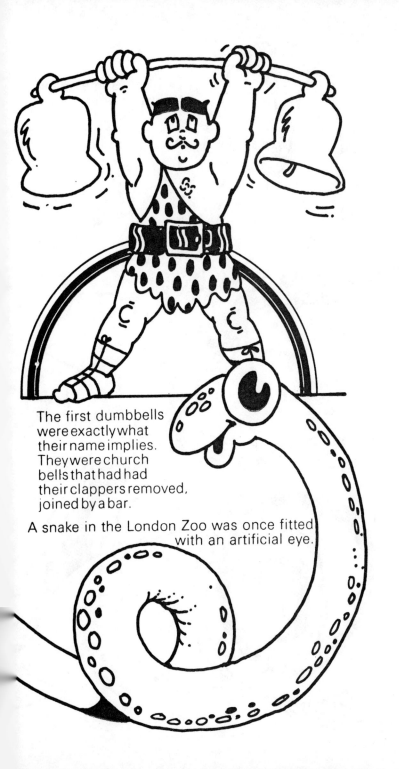

The first dumbbells were exactly what their name implies. They were church bells that had had their clappers removed, joined by a bar.

A snake in the London Zoo was once fitted with an artificial eye.

Some queen termites have been known to lay eggs for up to fifty years.

There have been ten years of war for every year of peace in world history.

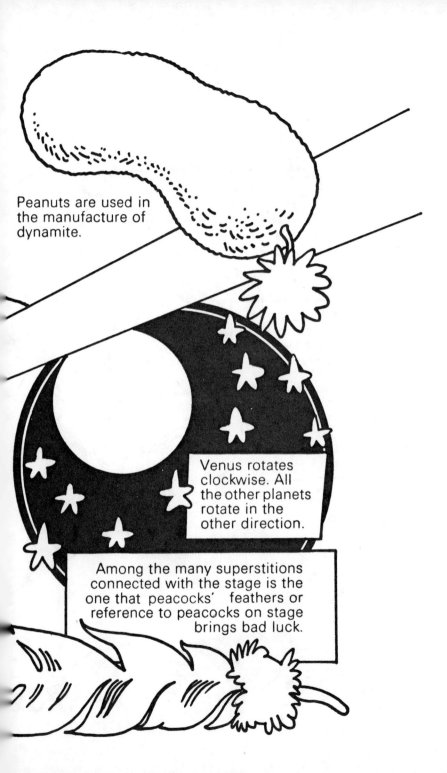

Peanuts are used in the manufacture of dynamite.

Venus rotates clockwise. All the other planets rotate in the other direction.

Among the many superstitions connected with the stage is the one that peacocks' feathers or reference to peacocks on stage brings bad luck.

In 1922 a
24-year-old
English woman
pleaded guilty
to 61
bigamous
marriages
which she had
made in the
space of five
years.

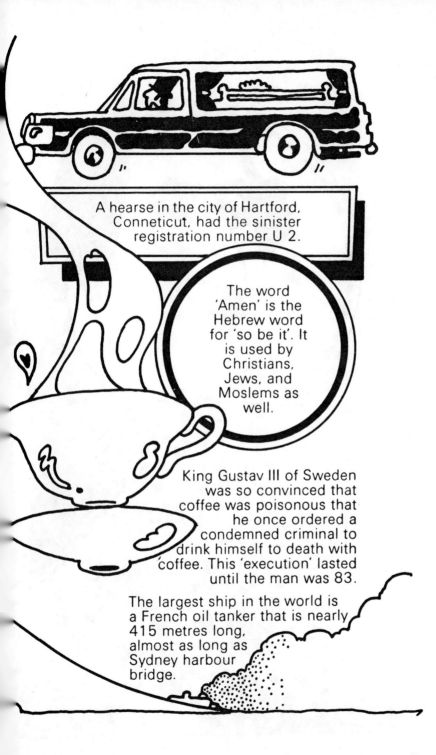

A hearse in the city of Hartford, Conneticut, had the sinister registration number U 2.

The word 'Amen' is the Hebrew word for 'so be it'. It is used by Christians, Jews, and Moslems as well.

King Gustav III of Sweden was so convinced that coffee was poisonous that he once ordered a condemned criminal to drink himself to death with coffee. This 'execution' lasted until the man was 83.

The largest ship in the world is a French oil tanker that is nearly 415 metres long, almost as long as Sydney harbour bridge.

The score of 'The Barber of Seville' was completed by Rossini in eight days.

The odds against a mother producing quadruplets are about 1 in 600,000

If a drop of whisky is squirted onto its back, a scorpion will sting itself to death.

The largest living plant, a redwood tree in California weighs over nine times as much as the largest animal that has ever lived, the Blue Whale.

The annual coal production of the USSR could supply London's current electricity needs for over 107 years.

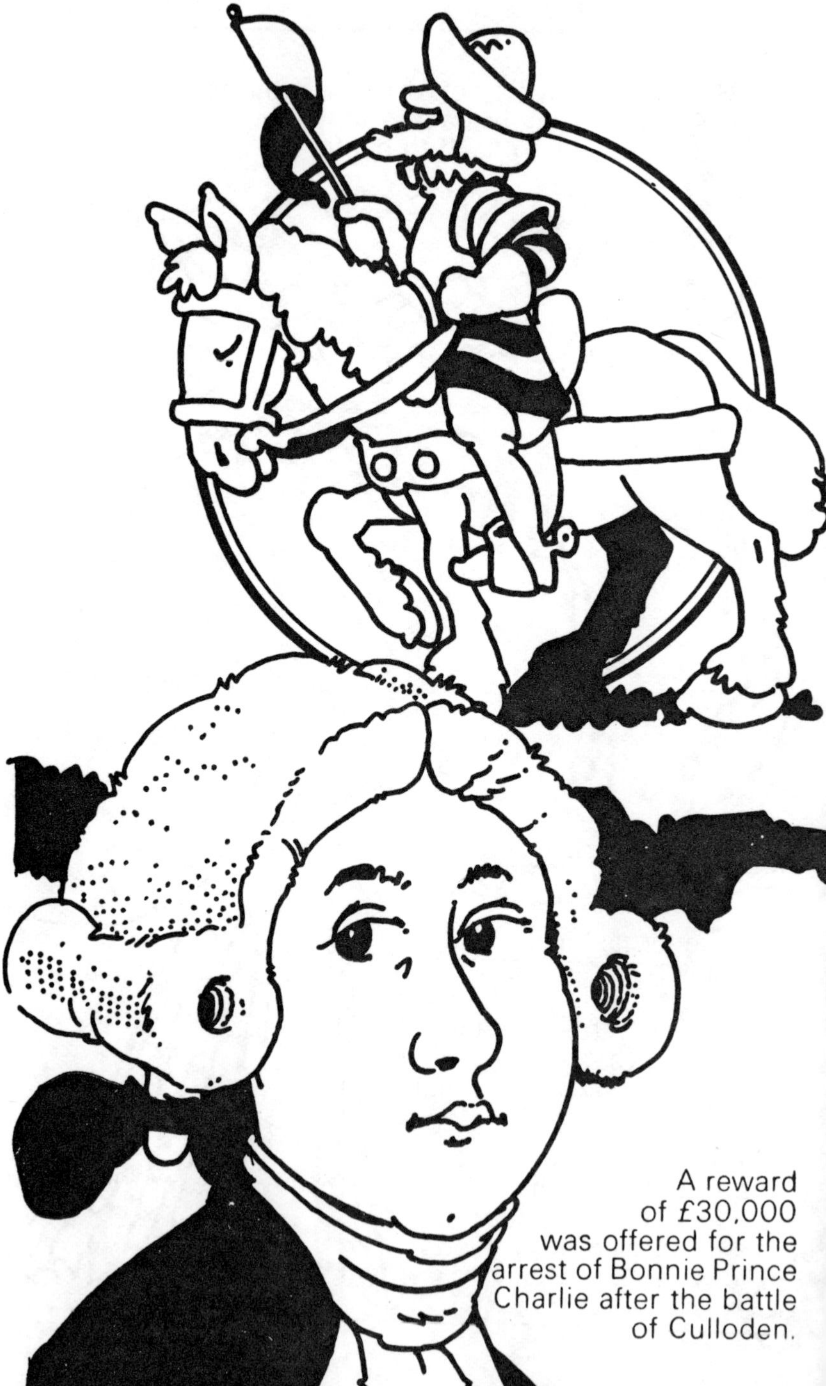

A reward
of £30,000
was offered for the
arrest of Bonnie Prince
Charlie after the battle
of Culloden.

Although
the horse
was a native
of the American
continent it died
out there about
10,000 years
ago and did not
reappear until it
was reintroduced
by the Spanish
during the
16th century.

The only miracle in
the New Testament
that is referred to by
all four evangelists
is the multiplication
of the loaves and the
fishes.

Seals only fall
asleep for
intervals of 1½
minutes.

It used to be
believed that
emeralds
helped women
in childbirth.

The income tax rate for the Gulf states of Bahrain, Kuwait and Qatar is nil.

Nearly every Moslem family has at least one child named after the prophet Mohammed, which makes it the most common first name in the world.

Jane Austen refers to baseball in her earliest full length novel 'Northanger Abbey'.

If you touch the leaves of the Sensitive Plant they will move away from you.

A French tennis champion called Charles Delhaye once played a tennis match clothed in the full uniform of the French national guard and carrying a pack and musket. He beat his more orthodoxly attired opponent 3 sets to 1.

191

Winds in the most powerful hurricanes can be 50 per cent more powerful than the average power of all the other winds blowing on earth at any one time.

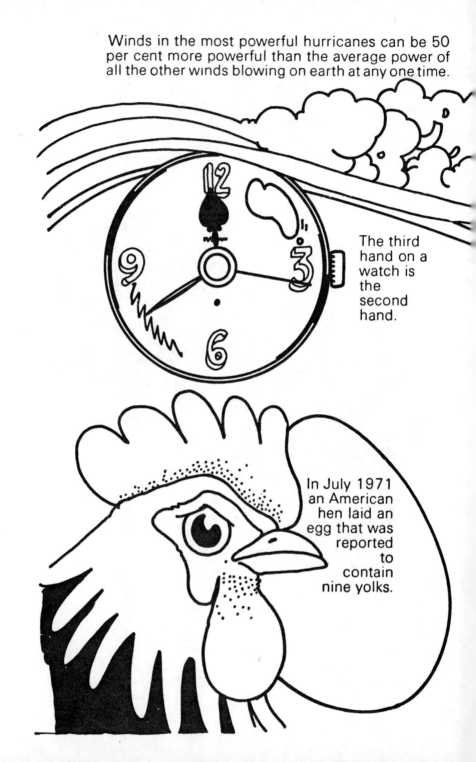

The third hand on a watch is the second hand.

In July 1971 an American hen laid an egg that was reported to contain nine yolks.

Any five digit number multiplied by 11 and then multiplied by 9091 will reappear twice in the product.

Whereas dogs wag their tails as a sign of welcome, cats wag theirs as a sign of warning.

The Egyptians kept dachshunds four thousand years ago.

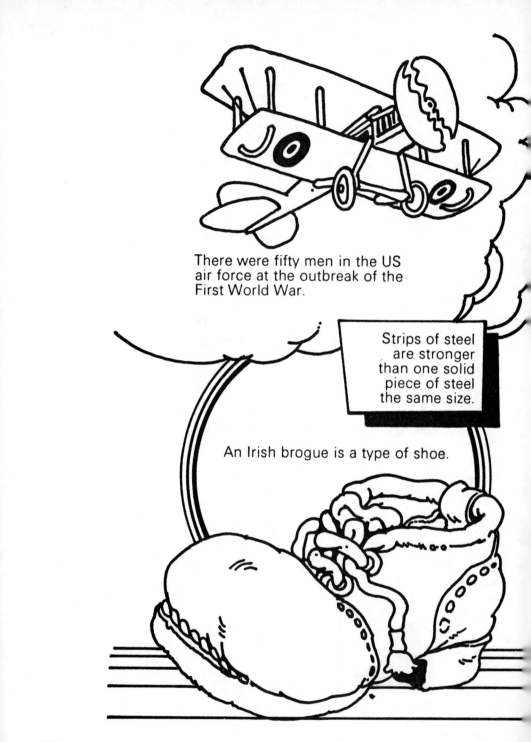

There were fifty men in the US air force at the outbreak of the First World War.

Strips of steel are stronger than one solid piece of steel the same size.

An Irish brogue is a type of shoe.

The Gaboon viper has fangs 50 mm long, the longest of any snake in the world.

The only apostle to die a natural death was St. John the Evangelist.

Tests have shown that the combination of black and yellow has the strongest visual impact, black on white follows next.

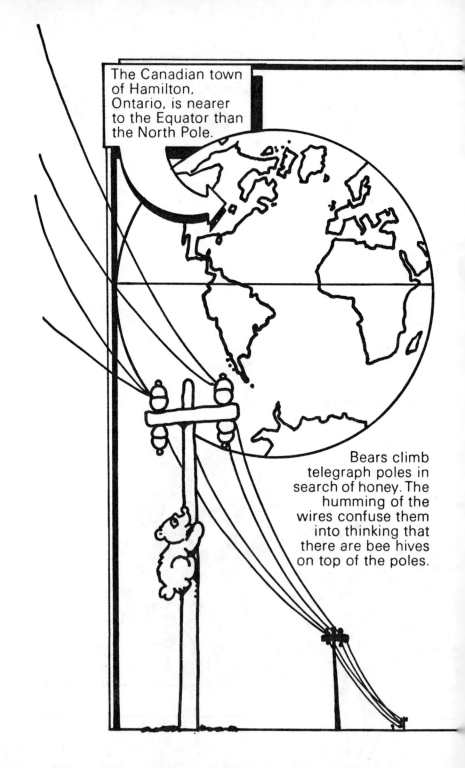

The Canadian town of Hamilton, Ontario, is nearer to the Equator than the North Pole.

Bears climb telegraph poles in search of honey. The humming of the wires confuse them into thinking that there are bee hives on top of the poles.

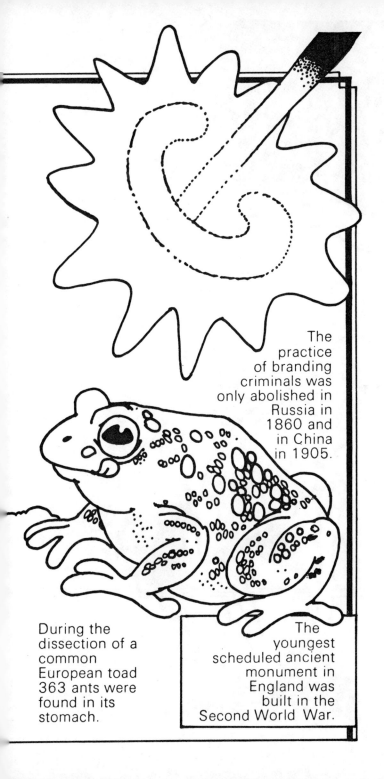

The
practice
of branding
criminals was
only abolished in
Russia in
1860 and
in China
in 1905.

During the
dissection of a
common
European toad
363 ants were
found in its
stomach.

The
youngest
scheduled ancient
monument in
England was
built in the
Second World War.

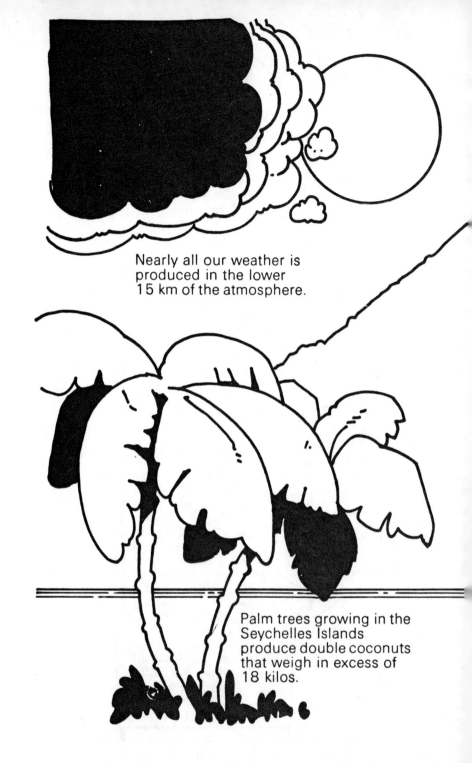

Nearly all our weather is produced in the lower 15 km of the atmosphere.

Palm trees growing in the Seychelles Islands produce double coconuts that weigh in excess of 18 kilos.

The largest sundial in the world is the Great Pyramid of Cheops in Egypt.

The nickname 'press' was first used to describe the publication of books.

An English billiards player called Henry Lewis could play with his nose, instead of a cue.

There is a lake on the Indonesian island of Java that blows bubbles into the air.

It takes a migrating English swallow about one month to fly to its wintering grounds in Africa.

A full moon is nine times brighter than a half moon.

The face patches worn by ladies in the 18th century not only aided their beauty, they indicated their political allegiances as well. Patches on the right side of the face showed support for the Whig cause, those on the left indicated Tory sympathies.

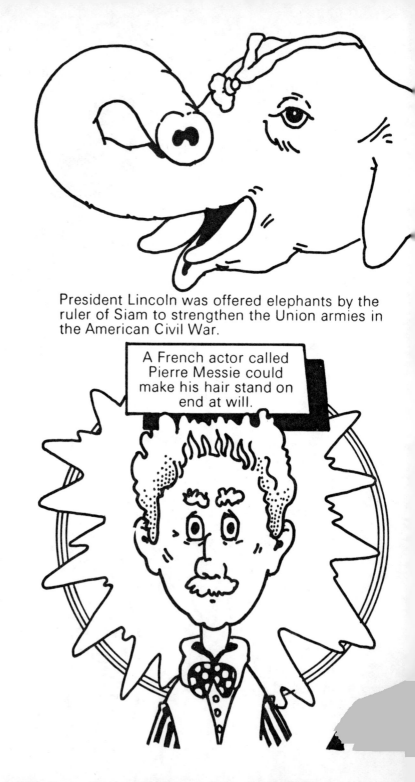

President Lincoln was offered elephants by the ruler of Siam to strengthen the Union armies in the American Civil War.

A French actor called Pierre Messie could make his hair stand on end at will.

The mangrove is one of the few trees that grows in salt water.

Winston Churchill was the first British Prime Minister to wear a uniform in office.

The word 'fathom' originated from an Anglo-Saxon word 'faethm' which meant an 'embrace'.

Eating mice that had been fried alive used to be regarded as a cure for smallpox in many parts of Britain.

Surgeons in ancient Egypt were liable to have their hands cut off if their patients died.

The value of the bank notes in circulation in England at the beginning of 1978 would have equalled a pile of £1 notes just over 744 km high.

The longest anyone has remained constipated is 102 days.

Many breeds of tropical fish could survive in an aquarium filled with human blood.

The jaguar catches fish with its paws.

During his lifetime Sir Isaac Newton wrote almost 100,000 pages of notes on alchemy, astrology and the occult.

The silkworm is not a worm. It is a caterpillar.

Richard
Wagner was
Franz Liszt's
son-in-law.

There is one
type of ice
that does not
melt - dry ice.
It evaporates.

The USSR is the greatest
consumer
of perfume in the world.

Arabic did not become generally spoken in Egypt until the 17th century.

Thousands of the quotations and references in the Oxford English Dictionary were submitted to the editor, Sir James Murray, by an inmate of Broadmoor, the asylum for mental criminals.

Overweight schoolchildren often eat less than their slimmer contemporaries.

Sir Arthur Conan Doyle worked as an ophthalmologist when he was not writing the Sherlock Holmes novels.

In 1975 chickens were employed to control traffic in a busy public park in Melbourne, Australia.

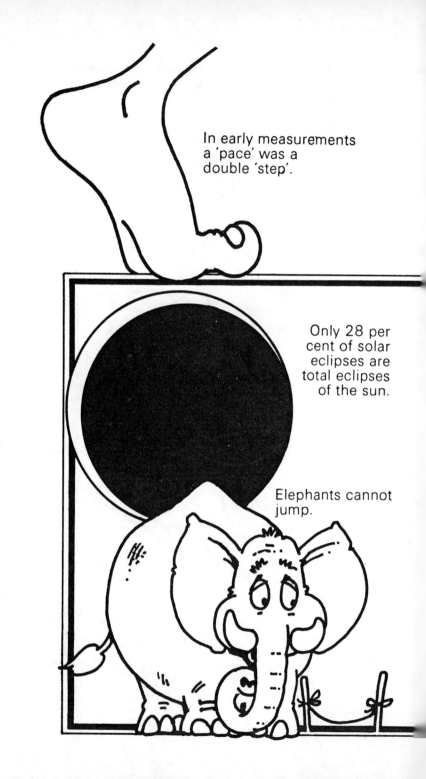

In early measurements a 'pace' was a double 'step'.

Only 28 per cent of solar eclipses are total eclipses of the sun.

Elephants cannot jump.

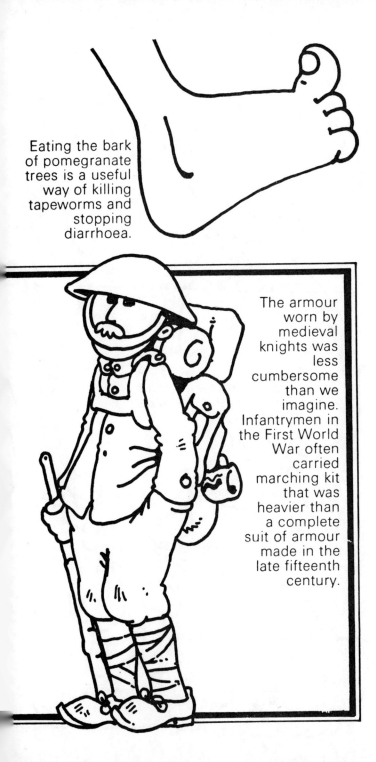

Eating the bark of pomegranate trees is a useful way of killing tapeworms and stopping diarrhoea.

The armour worn by medieval knights was less cumbersome than we imagine. Infantrymen in the First World War often carried marching kit that was heavier than a complete suit of armour made in the late fifteenth century.

Butterflies have their organs of taste located in their hind feet.

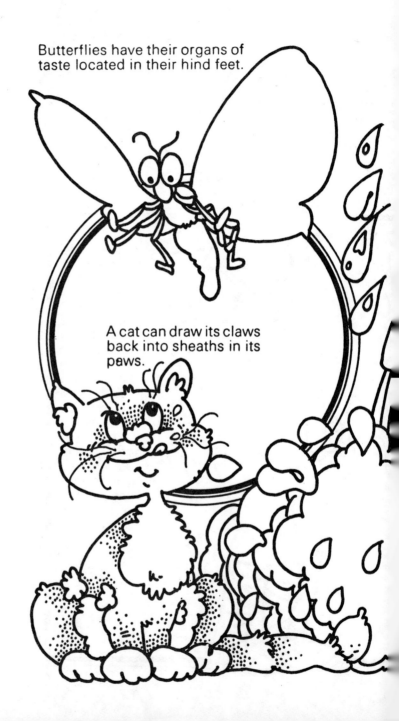

A cat can draw its claws back into sheaths in its paws.

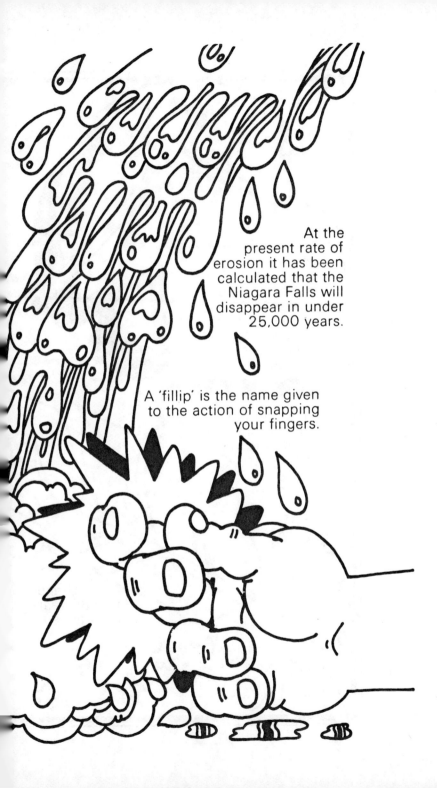

At the present rate of erosion it has been calculated that the Niagara Falls will disappear in under 25,000 years.

A 'fillip' is the name given to the action of snapping your fingers.

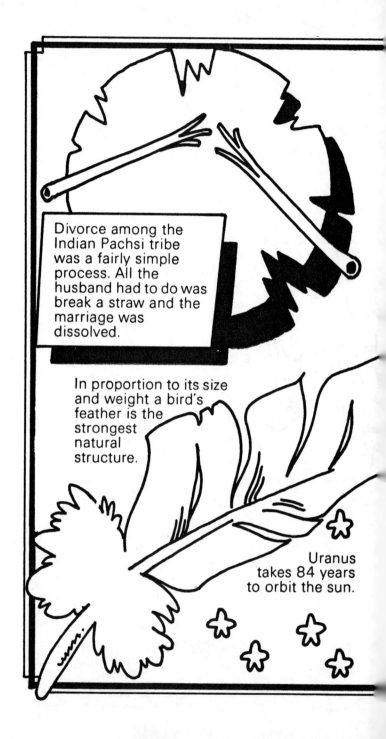

Divorce among the Indian Pachsi tribe was a fairly simple process. All the husband had to do was break a straw and the marriage was dissolved.

In proportion to its size and weight a bird's feather is the strongest natural structure.

Uranus takes 84 years to orbit the sun.

Weather vanes
face in the
opposite
direction to the
way the wind is
blowing.

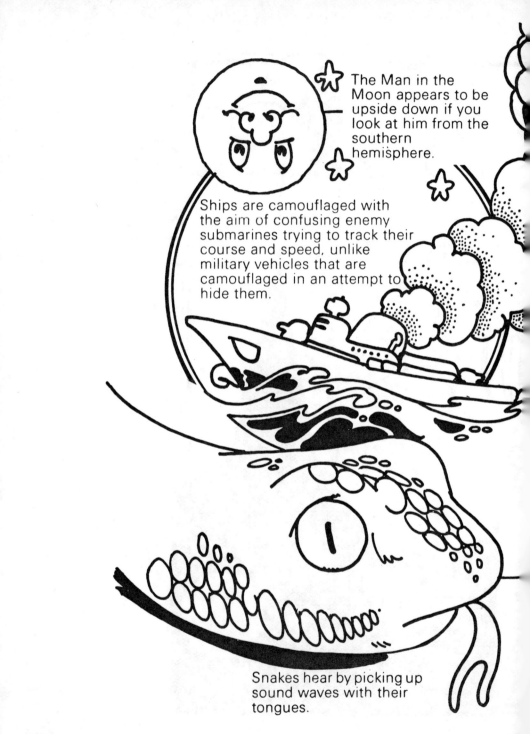

The Man in the Moon appears to be upside down if you look at him from the southern hemisphere.

Ships are camouflaged with the aim of confusing enemy submarines trying to track their course and speed, unlike military vehicles that are camouflaged in an attempt to hide them.

Snakes hear by picking up sound waves with their tongues.

The explosive charge of the first atom bomb was packed into a tube 7.6 cm long. When it exploded however, it had the same effect as 20,000 tonnes of TNT.

It is possible to mix oil and water. All you have to do is add a little soap.

Poodles do not moult.

There is a word in Aristophanes's play 'Ecclesiazusae' which contains 170 letters and means 'hash'.

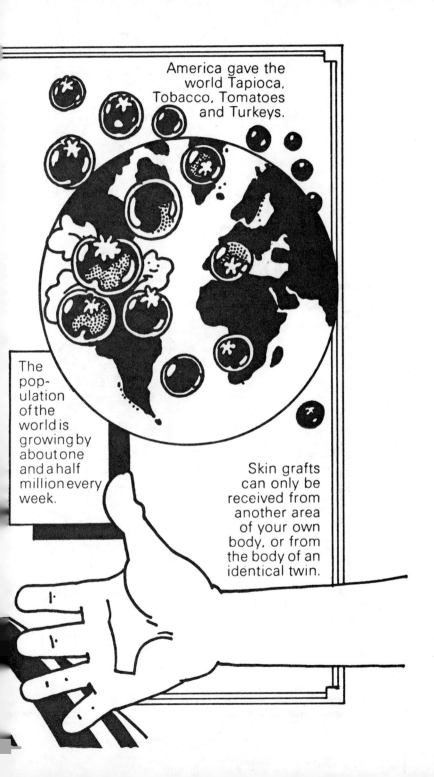

America gave the world Tapioca, Tobacco, Tomatoes and Turkeys.

The population of the world is growing by about one and a half million every week.

Skin grafts can only be received from another area of your own body, or from the body of an identical twin.

The doily is named after a seventeenth century English linen draper called Mr. Doiley.

'Why' is not only an interrogative word-it is a type of cow as well.

The late John Wayne was christened Marion Morrison.

Japanese cherry trees are grown purely for garden decoration and bear no fruit.

Two record breaking cars of the inter-war years, Sir Malcolm Campbell's 'Bluebird' and Sir Henry Segrave's 'Golden Arrow', were given the same aerodynamic shape as a tortoise.

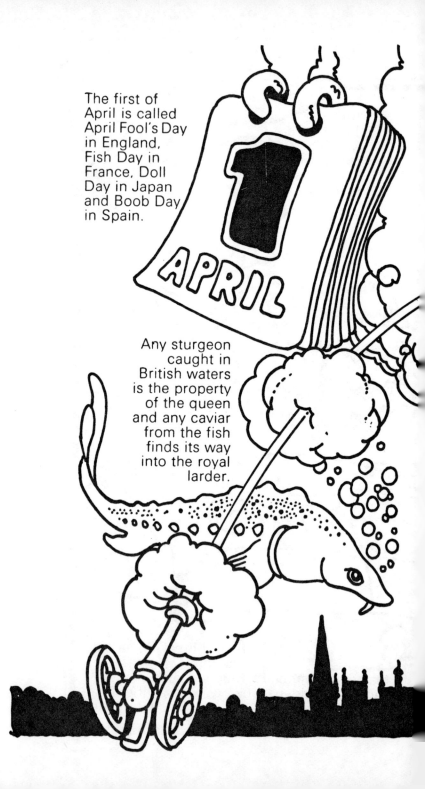

The first of April is called April Fool's Day in England, Fish Day in France, Doll Day in Japan and Boob Day in Spain.

Any sturgeon caught in British waters is the property of the queen and any caviar from the fish finds its way into the royal larder.

During the Franco-Prussian war the army used the first anti-aircraft gun. It was fired at French balloons.

Fireflies are not flies and glow-worms are not worms. They are all beetles.

All Soul's College, Oxford is the only educational institution that has never had students. The college has always consisted of fellows.

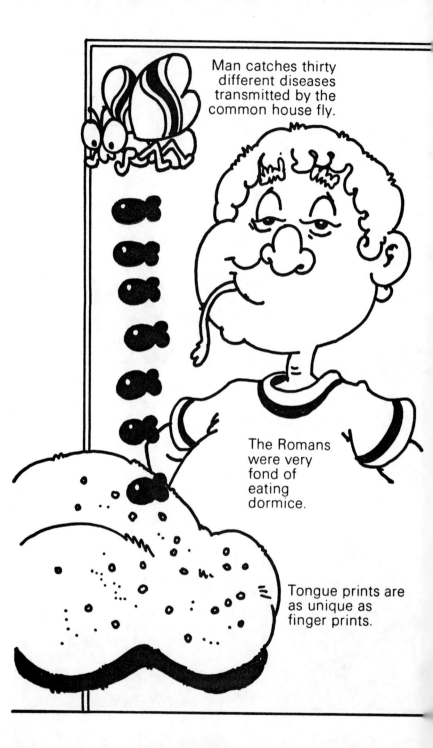

Man catches thirty different diseases transmitted by the common house fly.

The Romans were very fond of eating dormice.

Tongue prints are as unique as finger prints.

Benjamin Disraeli
was the first
British Prime
Minister to return
from Germany
bringing 'peace
with honour'.

The 'goose-step' was
first introduced into
the British Army.

The 'Red Lion' is the commonest pub name in Britain.

RED LION

It is possible to see both the Atlantic and the Pacific Oceans from the summit of Mt. Irazo, in Costa Rica.

There is a species of orchid that has pods which each hold about 70,000,000 tiny seeds.

The water pressure inside every onion cell would be sufficient to explode a steam engine.

$33 \times 3367 = 111{,}111$
$66 \times 3367 = 222{,}222$
$99 \times 3367 = 333{,}333$
$132 \times 3367 = 444{,}444$
etc. until you reach
$297 \times 3367 = 999{,}999$

Louis XIV took three baths in his lifetime, none of them voluntarily.

Sleeping babies are only six times less active than when they are awake.

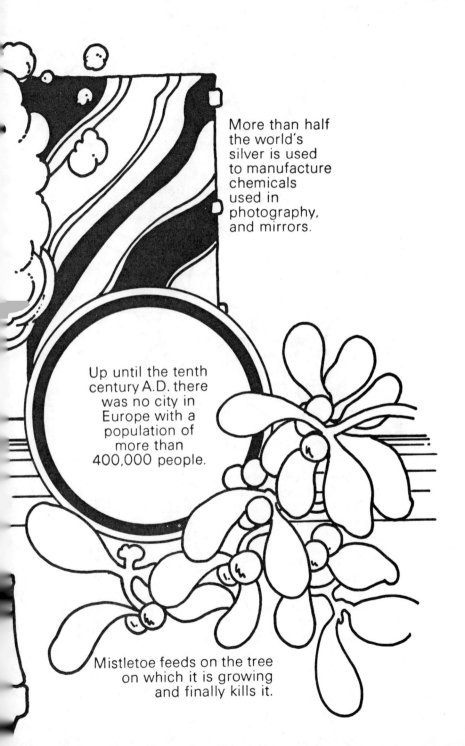

More than half the world's silver is used to manufacture chemicals used in photography, and mirrors.

Up until the tenth century A.D. there was no city in Europe with a population of more than 400,000 people.

Mistletoe feeds on the tree on which it is growing and finally kills it.

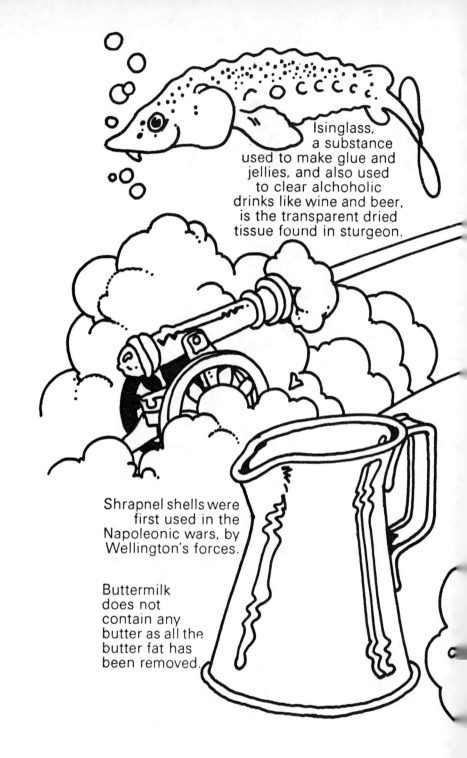

Isinglass, a substance used to make glue and jellies, and also used to clear alchoholic drinks like wine and beer, is the transparent dried tissue found in sturgeon.

Shrapnel shells were first used in the Napoleonic wars, by Wellington's forces.

Buttermilk does not contain any butter as all the butter fat has been removed.

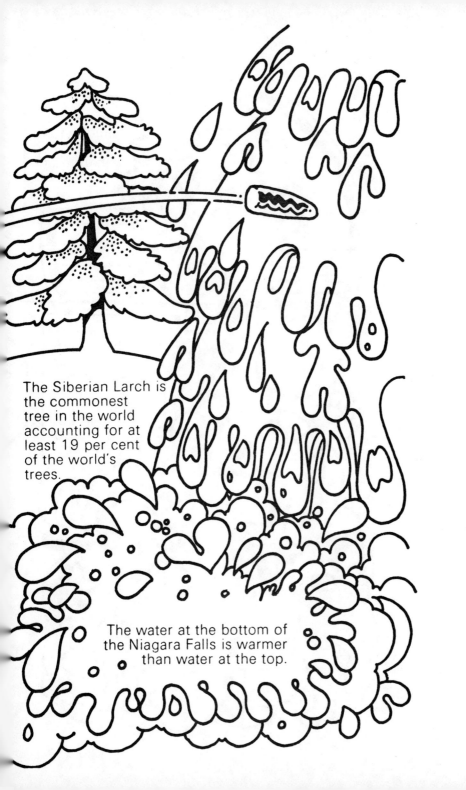

The Siberian Larch is the commonest tree in the world accounting for at least 19 per cent of the world's trees.

The water at the bottom of the Niagara Falls is warmer than water at the top.

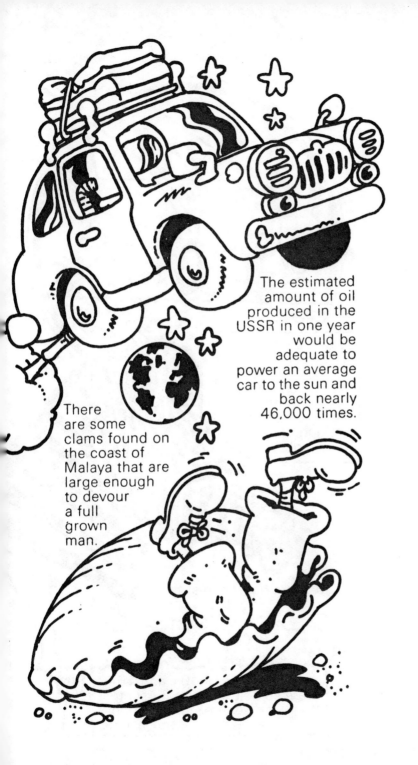

The estimated amount of oil produced in the USSR in one year would be adequate to power an average car to the sun and back nearly 46,000 times.

There are some clams found on the coast of Malaya that are large enough to devour a full grown man.

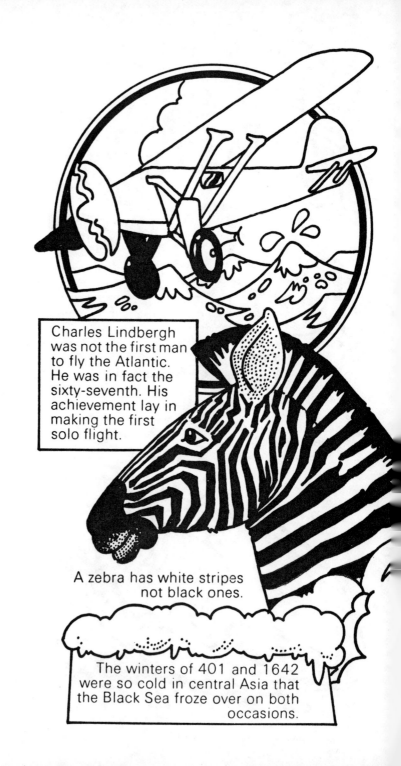

Charles Lindbergh was not the first man to fly the Atlantic. He was in fact the sixty-seventh. His achievement lay in making the first solo flight.

A zebra has white stripes not black ones.

The winters of 401 and 1642 were so cold in central Asia that the Black Sea froze over on both occasions.

A man called Al Cohol was once arrested in the American west coast city Seattle. He was charged with drunkenness.

If the leaves of ten Maple trees were spread out side by side they would cover an area of four hectares.

Turkish baths did not originate in Turkey nor are they baths. They are in fact hot-air rooms devised by the Romans.

Shooting stars are not stars, they
are meteors burning as
they descend through
the earth's
atmosphere.

The South Pole is nearer the sun
during the winter solstice in
December than any other part of
the earth.

There have only been three left-handed monarchs
on the English throne, James I, Queen Victoria
and George IV.

As a clock
unwinds it
loses weight.

THE CHALK
USED ON BLACK-
BOARDS IS MADE
FROM
PLASTER OF PARIS.

The average height of Frenchmen dropped after the Napoleonic wars as a result of the heavy casualties inflicted on Napoleon's forces and the emperor's practice of enlisting the tallest men.

There is a street in Canada that runs for a distance of nearly 1,900 kms.

A blind and handicapped Scotsman, William McPherson was able to read with his tongue.

The
Guinea-pig
is not a pig
and does
not come
from
Guinea. It
is a South
American
rodent.

The only animal that sleeps
on its back is man.

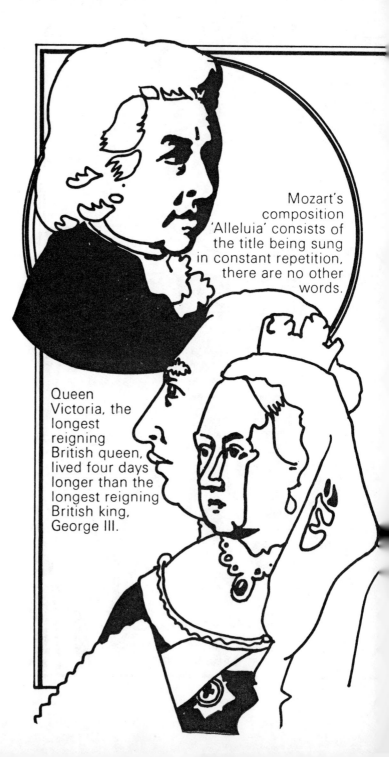

Mozart's composition 'Alleluia' consists of the title being sung in constant repetition, there are no other words.

Queen Victoria, the longest reigning British queen, lived four days longer than the longest reigning British king, George III.

A cow's moo was used as a unit of distance for more than two thousand years in India.

Spandau Prison in Berlin is maintained at an estimated cost of slightly less than a quarter of a million pounds every year to hold one captive, Rudolf Hess.

It takes over ten years
for a cork tree to grow
one layer of cork

Mosquitoes
prefer to bite
blondes.

One of the most
effective baits
for lobster-pots
is brick soaked
in
paraffin.

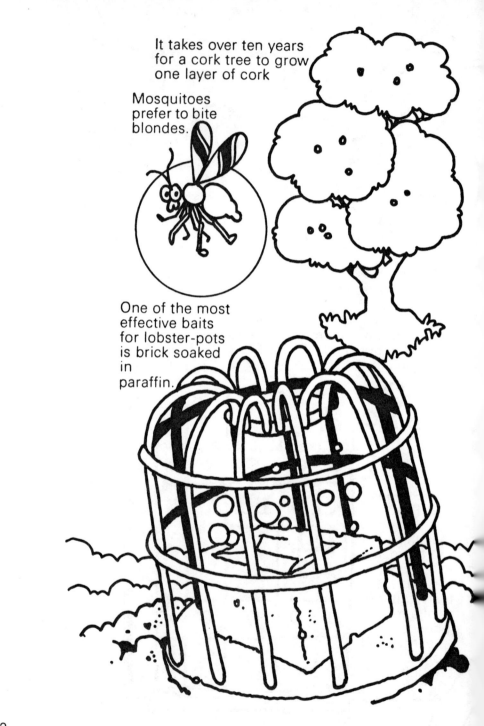

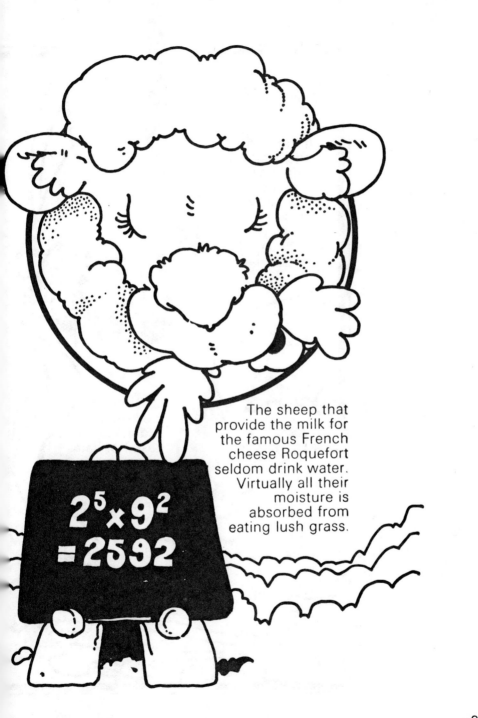

$$2^5 \times 9^2 = 2592$$

The sheep that provide the milk for the famous French cheese Roquefort seldom drink water. Virtually all their moisture is absorbed from eating lush grass.

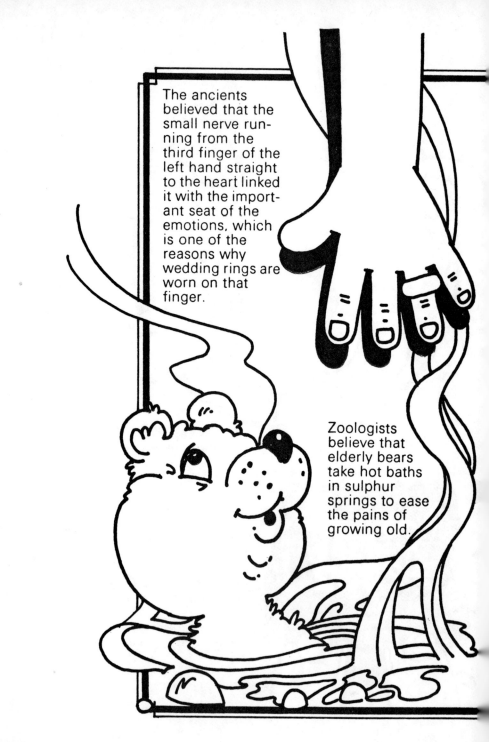

The ancients believed that the small nerve running from the third finger of the left hand straight to the heart linked it with the important seat of the emotions, which is one of the reasons why wedding rings are worn on that finger.

Zoologists believe that elderly bears take hot baths in sulphur springs to ease the pains of growing old.

Louis XIV developed a stomach twice the size of that of a normal man.

The parchment used to make drumskins comes from the skin of the ass.

The expression 'to eat humble pie' originated from a real pie made from the 'umbles' or less appetising inner parts of an animal.

An itemised list of repairs conducted in a Belgian Church included the following entries:'Renewing heaven, adjusting the stars and cleaning up the moon; decorating Noah's Ark and putting a head on Shem; mending the shirt of the prodigal son and cleaning his ear.'

The entire Roman world was auctioned by the Praetorian guard in 193 A.D. It raised the sum of £2,500,000.

An apple was called a napple at one time.

Most people move about forty times in their sleep during the night. Insomniacs may move as many as seventy times.

All the ants that you see working frantically in ant-armies are female.

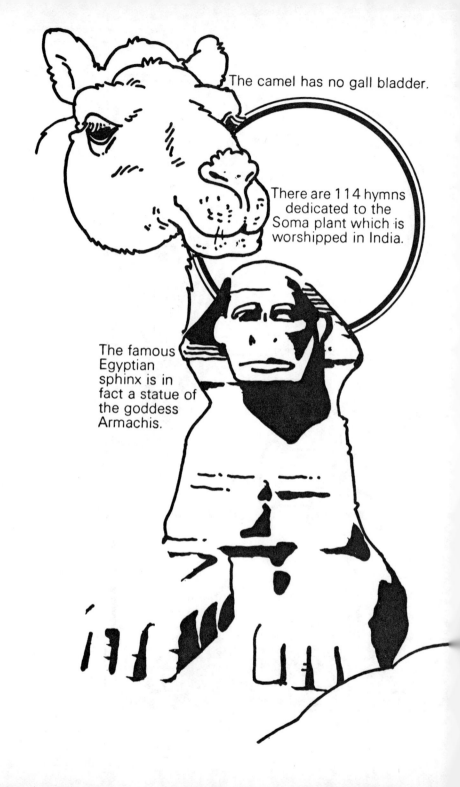

The camel has no gall bladder.

There are 114 hymns dedicated to the Soma plant which is worshipped in India.

The famous Egyptian sphinx is in fact a statue of the goddess Armachis.

In 1820 a man led his wife to the cattle market in Canterbury and sold her for five shillings (25p).

The first medical thermometers were so big and contained so much mercury that they needed five minutes to register the patient's temperature.

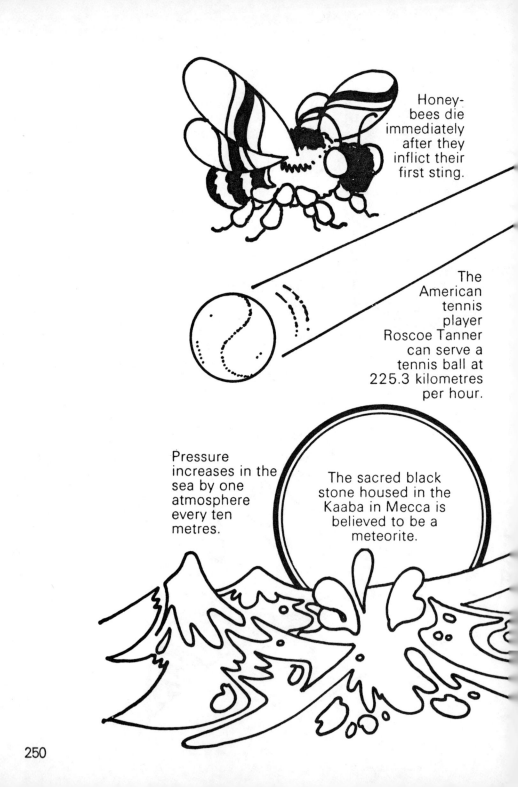

Honey-bees die immediately after they inflict their first sting.

The American tennis player Roscoe Tanner can serve a tennis ball at 225.3 kilometres per hour.

Pressure increases in the sea by one atmosphere every ten metres.

The sacred black stone housed in the Kaaba in Mecca is believed to be a meteorite.

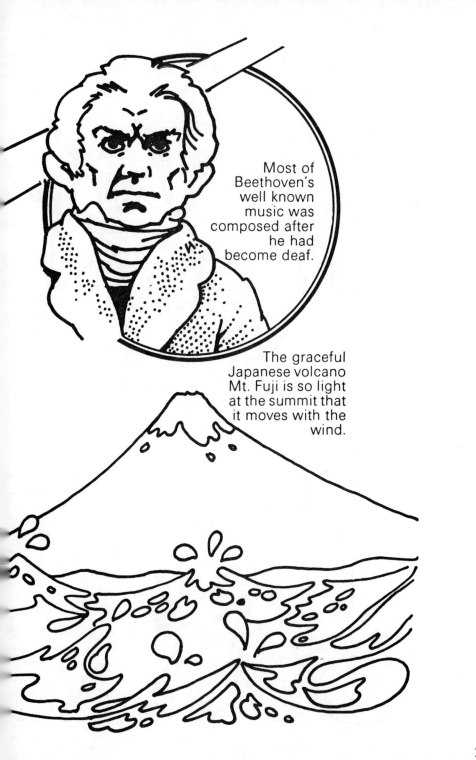

Most of Beethoven's well known music was composed after he had become deaf.

The graceful Japanese volcano Mt. Fuji is so light at the summit that it moves with the wind.

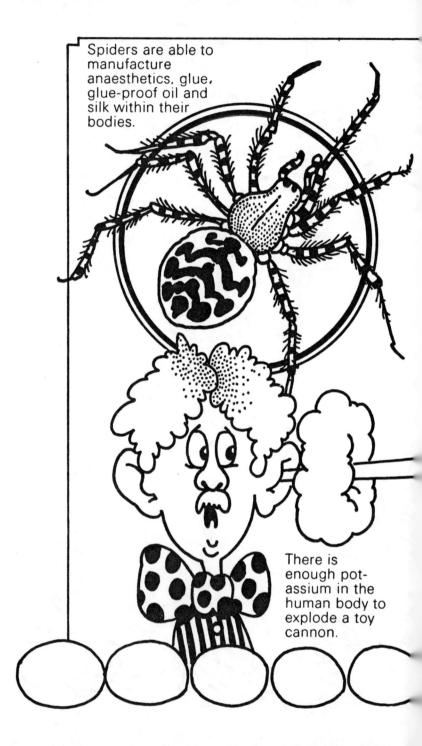

Spiders are able to manufacture anaesthetics, glue, glue-proof oil and silk within their bodies.

There is enough potassium in the human body to explode a toy cannon.

The sixteenth century French astrologer Nostradamus predicted the French Revolution, the rise of Fascist leaders like Hitler and Mussolini and the destruction of cities from the air.

The sphinx was carved from one piece of stone.

Every tenth egg is larger than the preceding nine.

King William IV of England was also William I of Hanover, William II of Ireland and William III of Scotland.

The Victorian organ virtuoso Sir Walter Parratt gave a concert at the age of twenty-one playing all the pieces from memory while he was playing two simultaneous games of chess behind his back. The concert was a great success and he managed to beat both his worthy opponents as well.

There are claimed to be more ghosts per square kilometre in England than in any other country on earth.

Soya beans are used in the manufacture of glue, paint, plastics and explosives.

On her second voyage to the New World the 'Mayflower' carried a cargo of slaves.

The pineapple is a berry and has nothing to do with pines or apples, except for its name.

In the earliest meanings of the words referring to someone as an 'uncouth idiot' was the same as calling them 'an unusual type of private individual' today.

256

Unlike imitation diamonds the real ones always feel cold.

Any whole number decreased by the sum of its digits will leave a remainder that can be divided by 9.

The Median prophet Zoroaster who founded the ancient fire-worshipping religion of Persia lived on nothing but cheese for thirty years.

It is possible for ferrets to catch colds in the same way that we do.

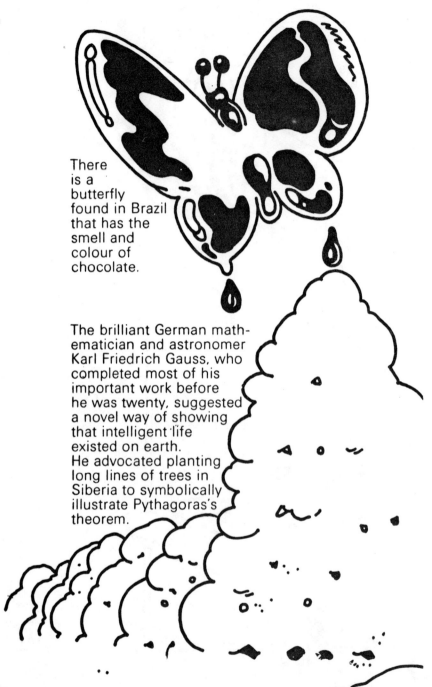

There
is a
butterfly
found in Brazil
that has the
smell and
colour of
chocolate.

The brilliant German mathematician and astronomer
Karl Friedrich Gauss, who
completed most of his
important work before
he was twenty, suggested
a novel way of showing
that intelligent life
existed on earth.
He advocated planting
long lines of trees in
Siberia to symbolically
illustrate Pythagoras's
theorem.

British barristers still wear black in mourning for the wife of William III, even though Queen Mary died in 1694.

There are at least eighty different varieties of rice grown in India.

An eccentric French heiress Madame de la Bresse left her fortune to be spent on buying clothes for snowmen.

Aircraft flying on the great circle routes have proved the shortest distance between two points on the earth's surface is not a straight line.

It is considered unwise to eat oysters in the months which do not have an R in their names, May, June, July and August.

An English author named Stephen Southwold predicted that the Second World War would break out on 3rd September 1939 in his book 'Valiant Clay' which was published in 1931.

The French
Empress Marie
Louise, who
married
Napoleon after
he had divorc-
ed Josephine,
possessed the
remarkable
ability of
moving her
ears at will and
even turning
them inside
out.

In 1696 a tiny
two-storey
church was built
inside a massive
oak tree in
Allouville, France.

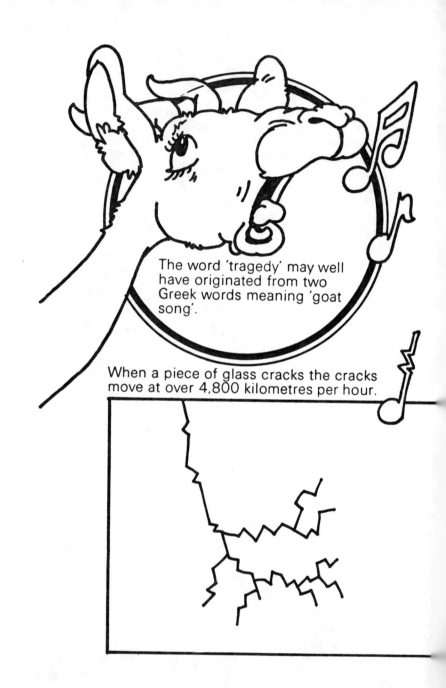

The word 'tragedy' may well have originated from two Greek words meaning 'goat song'.

When a piece of glass cracks the cracks move at over 4,800 kilometres per hour.

The super-stitions surrounding the number 13 originate from the Last Supper, when 13 sat down to eat.

Mercury, platinum, tungsten and uranium are all heavier than gold.

Every night a barn owl will eat more than its own weight in food. It later disposes of the pieces it can't man-age to eat.

Left-handed
playing cards
have pips in all
four corners.
Normal playing
cards have pips
in the top left-
hand corner
only.

The Empire State
Building in New
York City was built
to be able to with-
stand a sway
of 30 cm.
from the
perpendicular.

Lord Byron's boxing instructor, Gentleman Jackson, could sign his name with a 36 kilogramme weight balanced on his arm at the same time.

The lunar year has 354 days, the common year has 365 days and the Julian year has 365$\frac{1}{4}$ days.

A yak has the skeleton of a bison, the hair of a goat, the tail of a horse, the head of a cow and makes a grunt like a pig.

Water is hotter before boiling than when it has actually boiled.

In ancient Greece the symbol for a happy marriage was the triangle.

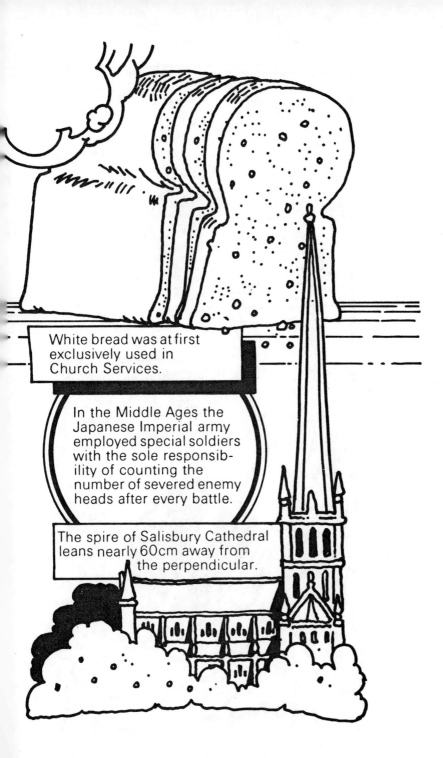

White bread was at first exclusively used in Church Services.

In the Middle Ages the Japanese Imperial army employed special soldiers with the sole responsibility of counting the number of severed enemy heads after every battle.

The spire of Salisbury Cathedral leans nearly 60cm away from the perpendicular.

The seventeenth king of Poland, John III, was born, crowned and married on the same day of the same month, June 17. Ironically he died on June 17 as well.

The original Cinderella was Egyptian.

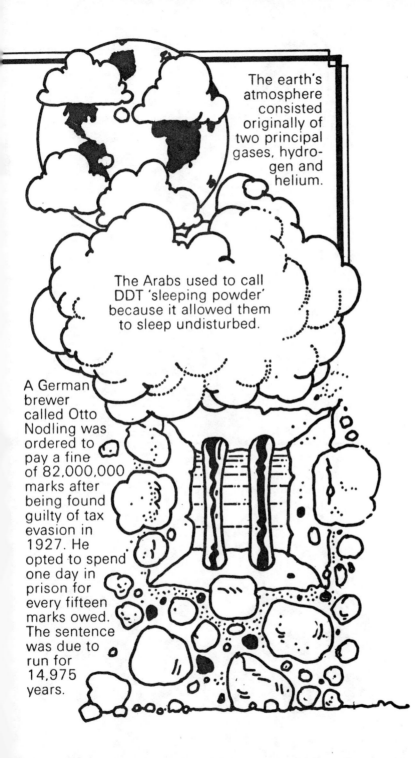

The earth's atmosphere consisted originally of two principal gases, hydrogen and helium.

The Arabs used to call DDT 'sleeping powder' because it allowed them to sleep undisturbed.

A German brewer called Otto Nodling was ordered to pay a fine of 82,000,000 marks after being found guilty of tax evasion in 1927. He opted to spend one day in prison for every fifteen marks owed. The sentence was due to run for 14,975 years.

Even though they look so fierce gorillas never kill in order to eat. They are strict vegetarians.

Fish has been served with a slice of lemon since the Middle Ages. Originally the lemon was intended to dissolve swallowed fish bones, only later did its effect on the taste become more important.

There is a church in Toronto, Canada, called the St. James Bond United church.

At birth our muscles are only one fortieth of their eventual size and power.

The foot-and-mouth epidemic in Britain of 1967-68 cost an estimated £150,000,000.

The smallest colony in the world is the Pacific Island of Pitcairn which has a population of under one hundred, who are principally Seventh Day Adventists.

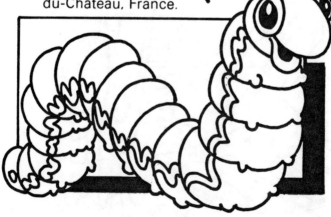

Ivory comes from the hippo- potamus, the walrus and the narwhal as well as from the elephant.

As recently as the 18th century caterpillars were excommunicated by a grand vicar of Pont- du-Château, France.

Birds are sometimes able to set their own broken wings.

The inventor of the compass, a Chinese called Chou Kung, had a hand which could swivel in a complete circle on the end of his wrist.

There is a waterfall near Honolulu which 'falls' upwards.

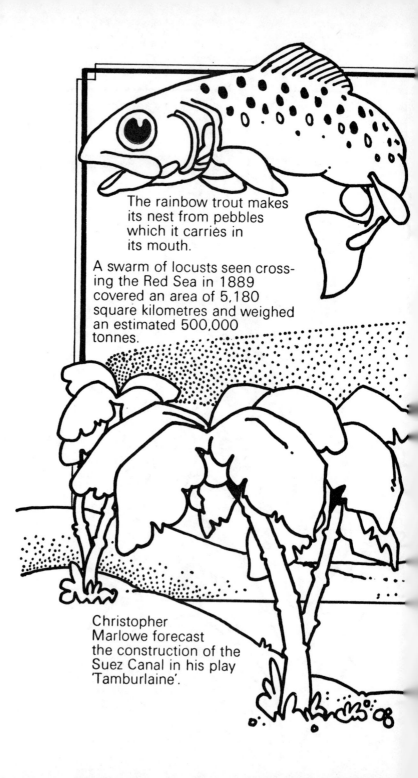

The rainbow trout makes its nest from pebbles which it carries in its mouth.

A swarm of locusts seen crossing the Red Sea in 1889 covered an area of 5,180 square kilometres and weighed an estimated 500,000 tonnes.

Christopher Marlowe forecast the construction of the Suez Canal in his play 'Tamburlaine'.

Queen Elizabeth I was the only British Sovereign between William I and Elizabeth II who did not effectively possess any land outside England and Wales.

In the state of Minnesota it is against the law to hang male and female underwear on the same washing-line.

A ship is between four and six times more efficient in converting energy into work than a duck.

80 per cent of the
population of
India live in
communities of
less than 5,000
inhabitants.

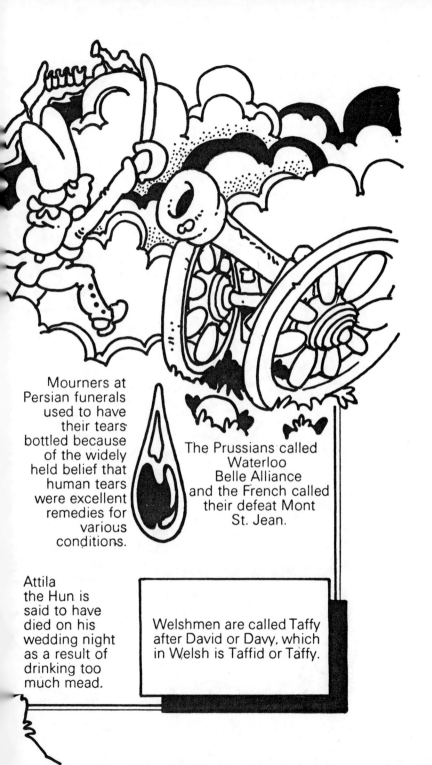

Mourners at Persian funerals used to have their tears bottled because of the widely held belief that human tears were excellent remedies for various conditions.

The Prussians called Waterloo Belle Alliance and the French called their defeat Mont St. Jean.

Attila the Hun is said to have died on his wedding night as a result of drinking too much mead.

Welshmen are called Taffy after David or Davy, which in Welsh is Taffid or Taffy.

With the exception of Antarctica all the continents are wider in the north than in the south.

The vapour trail from a comet with a mass of 250,070 cubic kilometres would weigh as much as the air you inhale in one breath.

37 cannot be divided by any other number but it will divide 111,222,333,444,555 etc. to 999.

During the siege of Delhi in 1296, the Moslem invader Ala-ud-Din was forced to use bags of gold as ammunition for his artillery.

The Chinese used to believe that eclipses were caused by the appetite of a hungry dragon.

The first gold brought back by Columbus was used to gild the ceiling of the church of Santa Maria Maggiore.

Homer
allegedly
died from
shame after
failing to
solve a riddle
put to him by some
fishermen. Homer
asked them how their
fishing was going to
which they replied,
'What we catch we
leave behind; what we
cannot catch we carry
away'. The answer is
fleas.

There are nearly 17,000
more people per square
kilometre in Monaco than
in Mongolia.

Divers who have been
breathing pure oxygen
for half an hour before a
descent have been able to
hold their breath under water
for thirteen minutes.

The twenty-first wife of Hieronymus of Rome had been married twenty times before.

The polecat was so named because it frequently fed on poultry. The French for a chicken is 'poule' and for cat is 'chat'.

Iron nails are never used to join oak because of the gallic acid in the wood which corrodes iron.

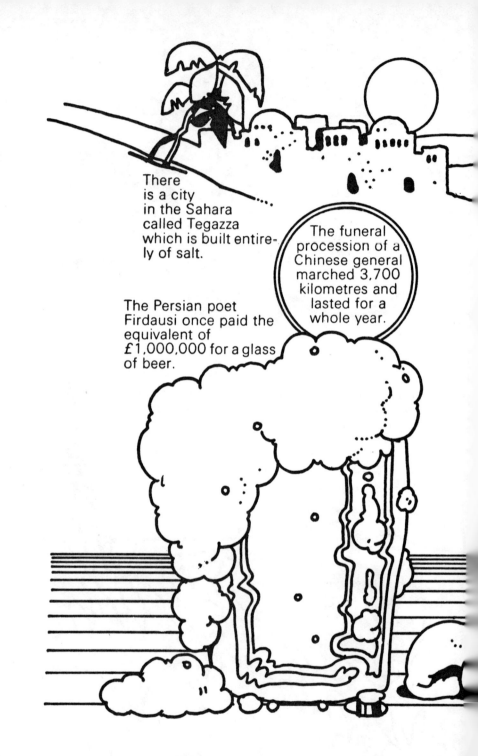

There is a city in the Sahara called Tegazza which is built entirely of salt.

The funeral procession of a Chinese general marched 3,700 kilometres and lasted for a whole year.

The Persian poet Firdausi once paid the equivalent of £1,000,000 for a glass of beer.

OBLIGE

There is no
word in English
that rhymes
with 'oblige'.

Seven normal sized men
could fit inside the coat
of Brobdingnagian
Bright.

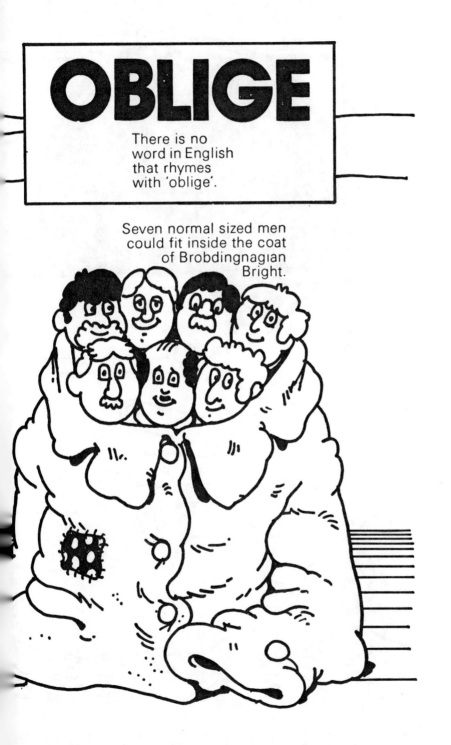

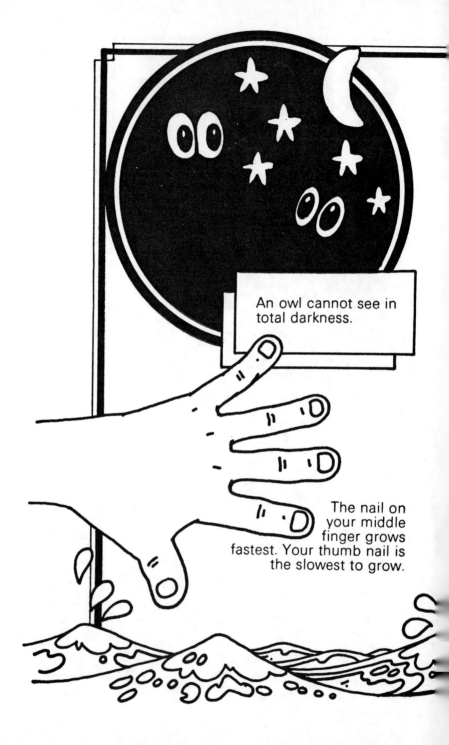

An owl cannot see in total darkness.

The nail on your middle finger grows fastest. Your thumb nail is the slowest to grow.

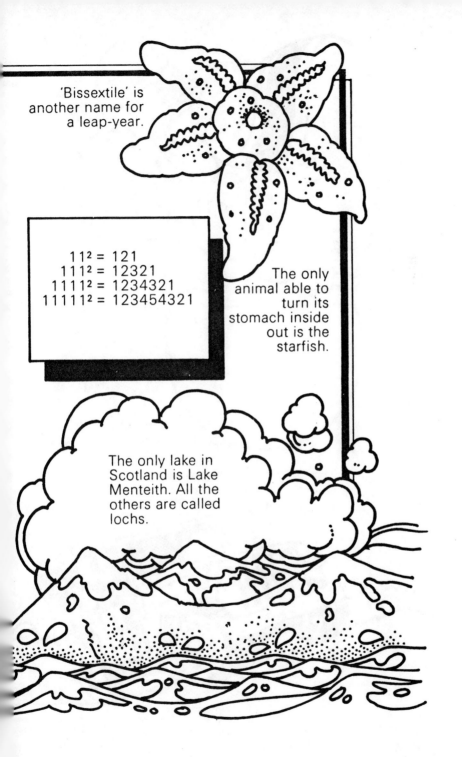

'Bissextile' is another name for a leap-year.

$11^2 = 121$
$111^2 = 12321$
$1111^2 = 1234321$
$11111^2 = 123454321$

The only animal able to turn its stomach inside out is the starfish.

The only lake in Scotland is Lake Menteith. All the others are called lochs.

A queen bee only leaves her hive to lead out a swarm and to go on her wedding flight.

One of the moons of Mars called Deimos rises and sets twice a day.

The Jeep got its name from its original initials G.P., which stood for General Purpose vehicle.

The bells that are tolled at funerals and the shots that are fired at military burials are Christian adaptations of pagan practices of frightening away evil spirits.

François I, King of France, banned the wearing of whiskers on pain of death.

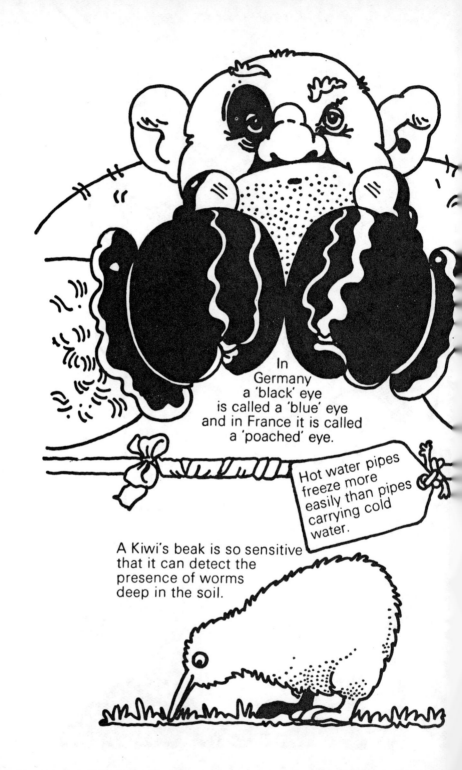

In Germany a 'black' eye is called a 'blue' eye and in France it is called a 'poached' eye.

Hot water pipes freeze more easily than pipes carrying cold water.

A Kiwi's beak is so sensitive that it can detect the presence of worms deep in the soil.

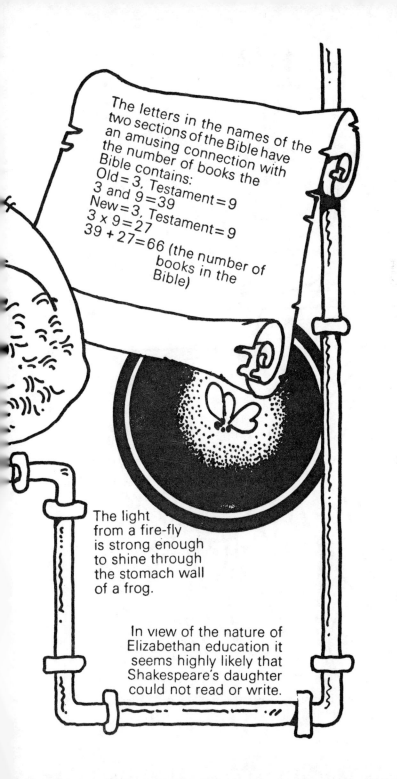

The letters in the names of the two sections of the Bible have an amusing connection with the number of books the Bible contains:

Old = 3, Testament = 9
3 and 9 = 39
New = 3, Testament = 9
3 × 9 = 27
39 + 27 = 66 (the number of books in the Bible)

The light from a fire-fly is strong enough to shine through the stomach wall of a frog.

In view of the nature of Elizabethan education it seems highly likely that Shakespeare's daughter could not read or write.

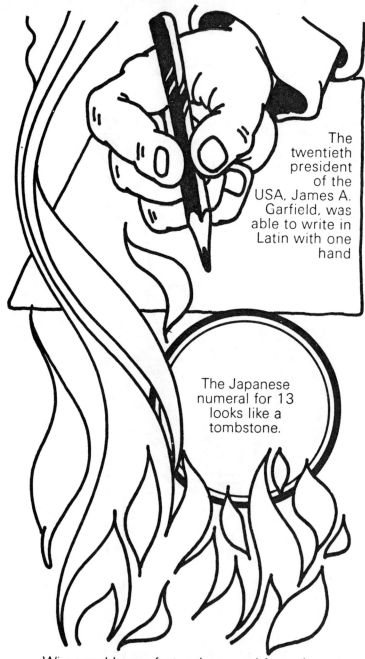

The twentieth president of the USA, James A. Garfield, was able to write in Latin with one hand

The Japanese numeral for 13 looks like a tombstone.

Wire wool burns faster than wool from the sheep's back.

while simultaneously writing in Greek with the other.

When 'anathema' is used with the stress on the second syllable it means 'cursed'. Spoken with the stress on the third syllable the mean-changes, though, to 'a divine object'.

The size of hats is determined by measuring the maximum length and breadth of the head, adding the results together and then dividing them by two.

The longest one word palindrome in English is 'redivider', which spells the same word reading the letters either forwards or backwards.

There is a speaking well in the village of Troo, Montoire, France, which repeats whole phrases spoken into it.

Sea otters have not one, but two coats of fur.

The 'chadouf' or water-raising song has been sung along the banks of the Nile for about 5,000 years.

One of the Moorish Kings of Spain, Abbad el Motaddid of Seville, used the skulls of enemies he had personally killed as flower pots.

On average more snow falls in the State of Virginia, in the eastern part of the USA, than in the Arctic lowlands.

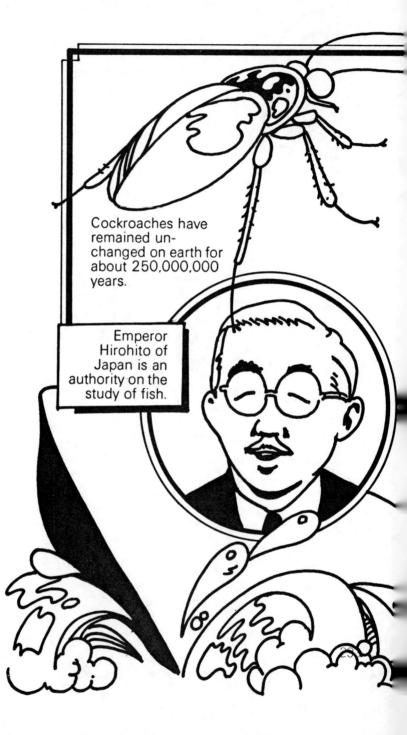

Cockroaches have remained un-changed on earth for about 250,000,000 years.

Emperor Hirohito of Japan is an authority on the study of fish.

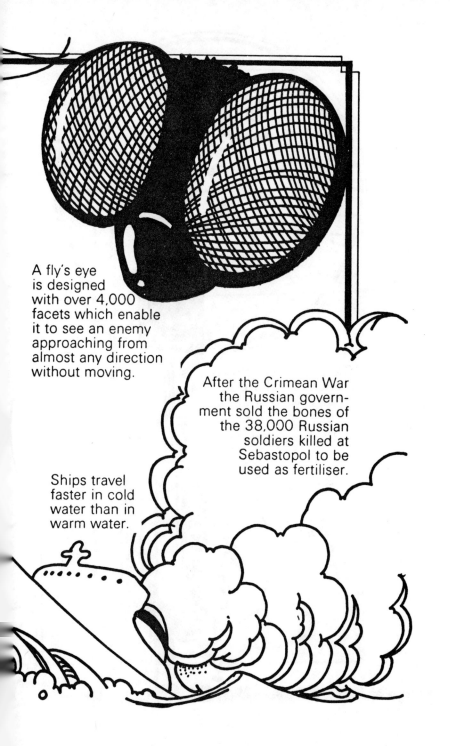

A fly's eye is designed with over 4,000 facets which enable it to see an enemy approaching from almost any direction without moving.

After the Crimean War the Russian government sold the bones of the 38,000 Russian soldiers killed at Sebastopol to be used as fertiliser.

Ships travel faster in cold water than in warm water.

The Sequeru cactus grows
branches that are sixteen
times taller than a man.

The so-called Prairie
dog is a rodent.

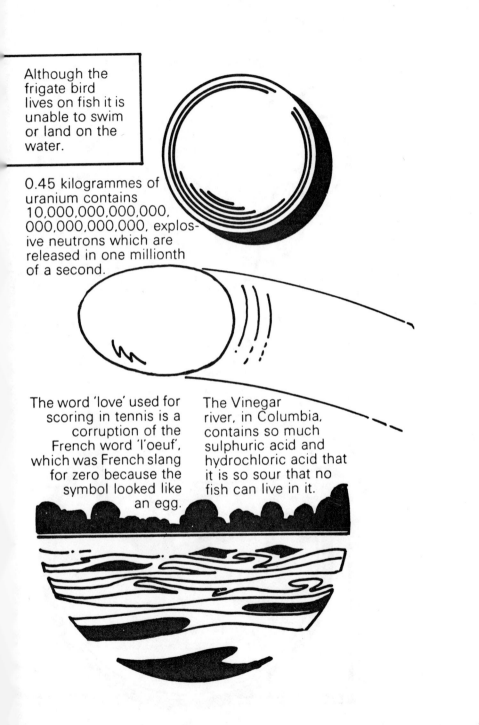

Although the frigate bird lives on fish it is unable to swim or land on the water.

0.45 kilogrammes of uranium contains 10,000,000,000,000, 000,000,000,000, explosive neutrons which are released in one millionth of a second.

The word 'love' used for scoring in tennis is a corruption of the French word 'l'oeuf', which was French slang for zero because the symbol looked like an egg.

The Vinegar river, in Columbia, contains so much sulphuric acid and hydrochloric acid that it is so sour that no fish can live in it.

In Korea you can buy eggs by the string.

According to the Acts of the Apostles the followers of Jesus Christ were first given the name Christians in Antioch, now in Turkey.

The possible distributions of hands in a game of bridge amount to a total of 53,644,737,765,488, 792,839,237,440,000.

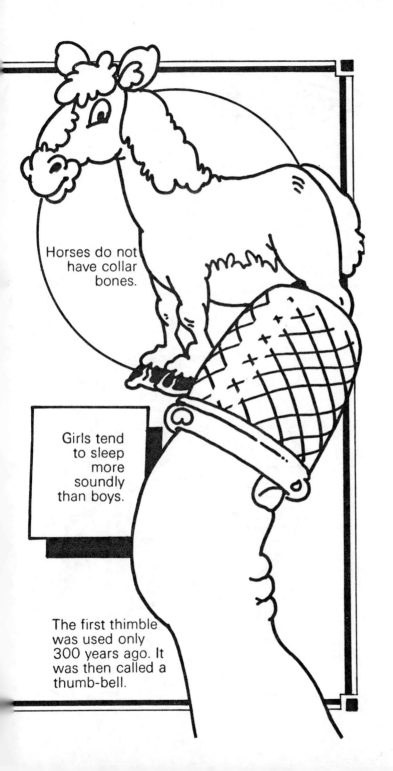

Horses do not have collar bones.

Girls tend to sleep more soundly than boys.

The first thimble was used only 300 years ago. It was then called a thumb-bell.

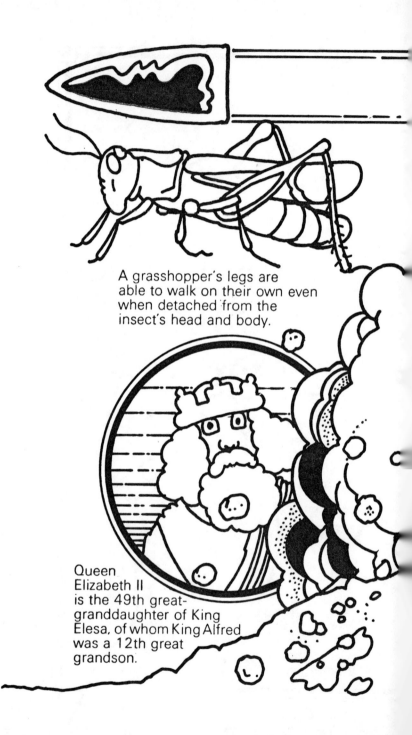

A grasshopper's legs are able to walk on their own even when detached from the insect's head and body.

Queen Elizabeth II is the 49th great-granddaughter of King Elesa, of whom King Alfred was a 12th great grandson.

The speed at which the earth revolves around the sun is roughly eight times faster than that at which a bullet leaves a gun.

A human hair laid on a bar of steel and then passed through a cold rolling mill would leave an imprint on the face of the steel.

A fortnight after the English opera singer Elizabeth Billington gave a stunning performance in Naples in 1794 she was blamed by the Neapolitans for causing an eruption of Vesuvius.

Some lichen are able to absorb half their own weight in water in ten minutes.

A Parisian music teacher, Alphonse Durand, christened seven of his children Do, Re Mi, Fa, Sol, La and Si. The eighth child was named Octave.

When you toasted a lady's health in ancient Rome it was customary to drink one glass for every letter of her name.

For several years Aurélien School published a rubber newspaper for the benefit of those who enjoyed reading it in their baths.

The shapes of letters O,B,P and F reflect the shape of the mouth when the sounds are made. O indicates an open mouth. B is the profile of sealed lips pronouncing it. P shows the lips partly open and F is the P shape but with the air escaping to make the F sound.

In 1910 there was an outbreak of the plague in Sussex.

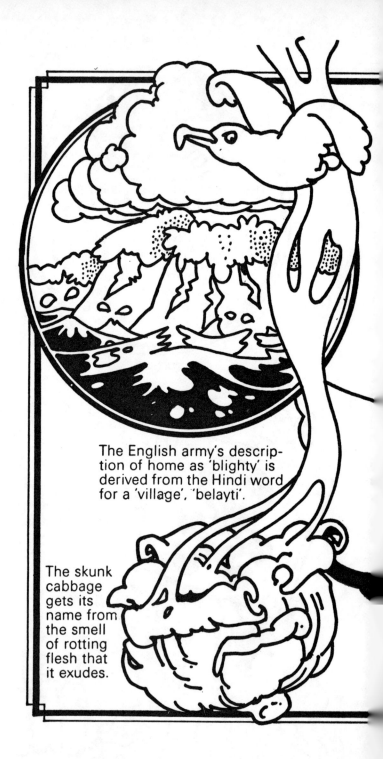

The English army's description of home as 'blighty' is derived from the Hindi word for a 'village', 'belayti'.

The skunk cabbage gets its name from the smell of rotting flesh that it exudes.

Monarch butterflies migrate more than 3,000 kilometres every year.

The actor Danny Kaye made his stage debut in the part of a watermelon seed.

The Etruscans were the first to use the eagle as a symbol of royal power.

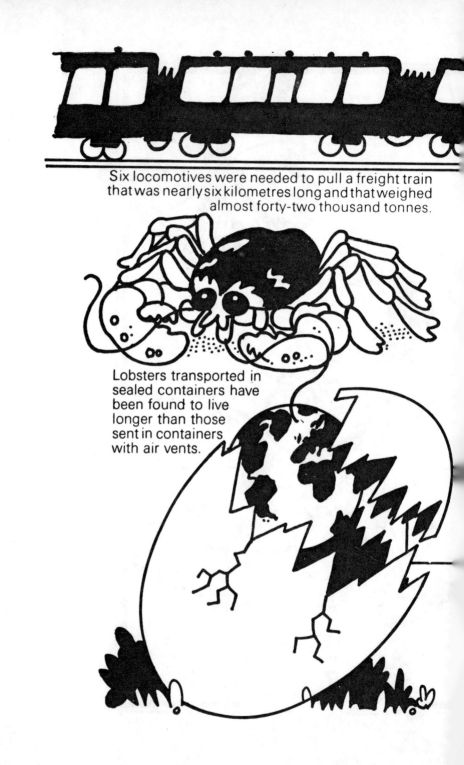

Six locomotives were needed to pull a freight train that was nearly six kilometres long and that weighed almost forty-two thousand tonnes.

Lobsters transported in sealed containers have been found to live longer than those sent in containers with air vents.

The rings round Saturn are about 80,500 kilometres in circumference but only about 30 centimetres thick.

The ancient Egyptians believed that the world was hatched from an egg laid by the sacred ibis.

French artist Anne-Louis Girodet only painted at night by the light of forty candles stuck in the brim of his hat. He based his fees on the number of candles burned in the painting of every picture.

It takes a cicada 17 years to develop as a larva, but its adult life only lasts four weeks.

A Chamois can stand on an area not much larger than a 50p piece.

In Madagascar the silk from spiders' webs is woven into a cloth.

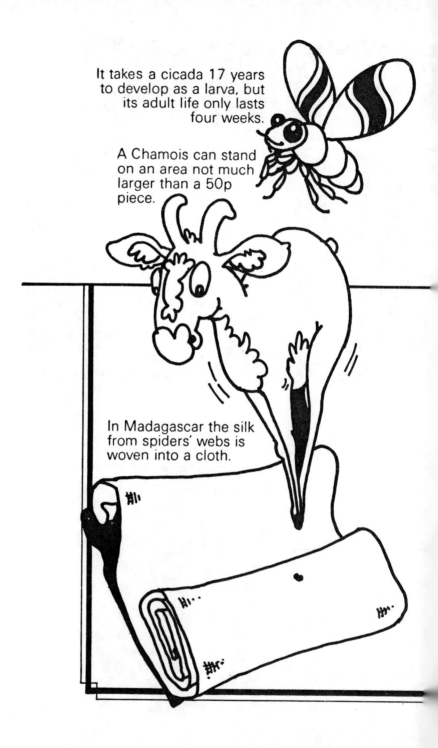

The fear of beds is known as 'clinophobia'.

Frau Sophie Bunnen, wife of a Prussian farmer, was reported to have given birth to eleven children in sixteen months. She produced sextuplets and quintuplets.

There is one acupuncture point in your body for each of the following conditions: boils, alcoholism and nympho-mania.

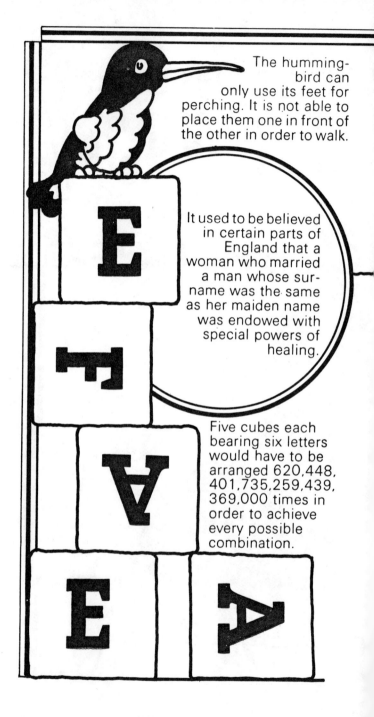

The humming-bird can only use its feet for perching. It is not able to place them one in front of the other in order to walk.

It used to be believed in certain parts of England that a woman who married a man whose sur-name was the same as her maiden name was endowed with special powers of healing.

Five cubes each bearing six letters would have to be arranged 620,448, 401,735,259,439, 369,000 times in order to achieve every possible combination.

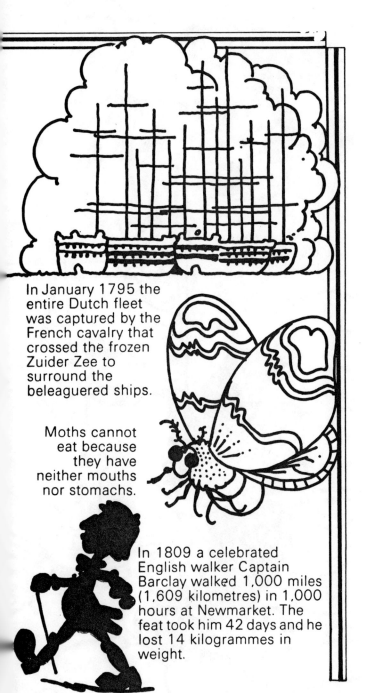

In January 1795 the entire Dutch fleet was captured by the French cavalry that crossed the frozen Zuider Zee to surround the beleaguered ships.

Moths cannot eat because they have neither mouths nor stomachs.

In 1809 a celebrated English walker Captain Barclay walked 1,000 miles (1,609 kilometres) in 1,000 hours at Newmarket. The feat took him 42 days and he lost 14 kilogrammes in weight.

The only naturally blue food is the Irish Bilberry.

All those wishing to be elected to official positions in ancient Rome used to wear white togas before the elections took place. The Latin word for 'white', 'candidus' gives us our word 'candidate'.

The Boya bird which is found in the Philippines weaves fireflies into its nest causing it to glow in the dark.

Johann Georg Krünitz wrote an encyclopaedia containing 242 volumes entirely in longhand.

A pythoness is a witch, not a female snake as might be expected.

A medium sized swarm of locusts contains about one million insects and consumes about twenty tonnes of food a day.

The 'primrose' has nothing to do with roses. It is named after the French phrase 'primes rolles' meaning 'earliest little flowers'. The Old French word 'primerose' was the name given to what we now call a 'hollyhock'.

Military bugle calls were introduced into all sections of the army in the middle of the eighteenth century. The first publication of bugle calls appeared in 1798 and it is possible that some of these were composed by Emperor Franz Joseph who happened to be in Britain at the time.

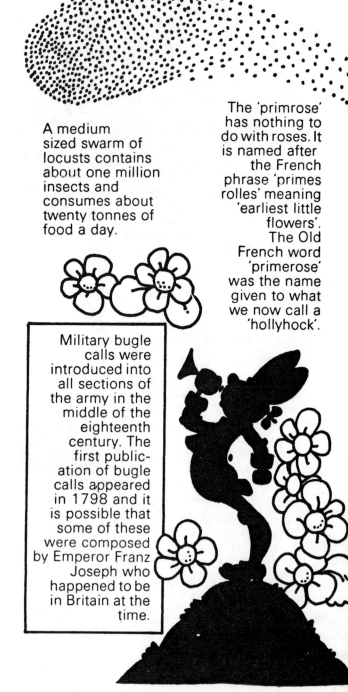

The question mark ?
developed from the
early practice of
putting the first and
last letters of the
word 'questio' after
a sentence. As this
practice increased
the 'q' was written
above the 'o', until
finally the 'q' degen-
erated into ? and the
'o' became simply . .

The
first
person
reported
to have
committed
suicide by fall-
ing onto his
own sword was
King Saul.

In correct heraldic terminology the American flag should not be called the 'Stars and Stripes', it should be the 'Mullets and Barrulets.'

General Eisenhower is reported to have owned a pair of pyjamas that contained the five stars of his rank on the lapels.

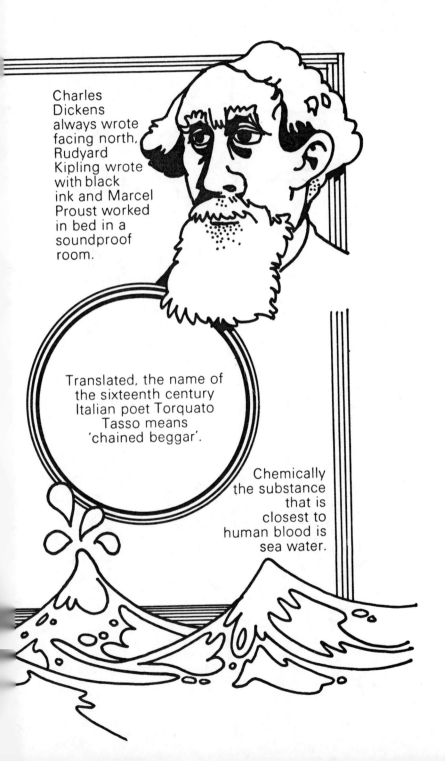

Charles Dickens always wrote facing north, Rudyard Kipling wrote with black ink and Marcel Proust worked in bed in a soundproof room.

Translated, the name of the sixteenth century Italian poet Torquato Tasso means 'chained beggar'.

Chemically the substance that is closest to human blood is sea water.

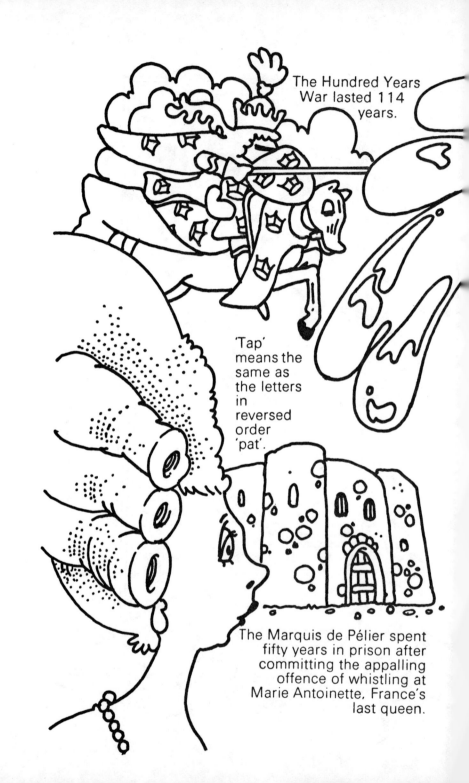

The Hundred Years War lasted 114 years.

'Tap' means the same as the letters in reversed order 'pat'.

The Marquis de Pélier spent fifty years in prison after committing the appalling offence of whistling at Marie Antoinette, France's last queen.

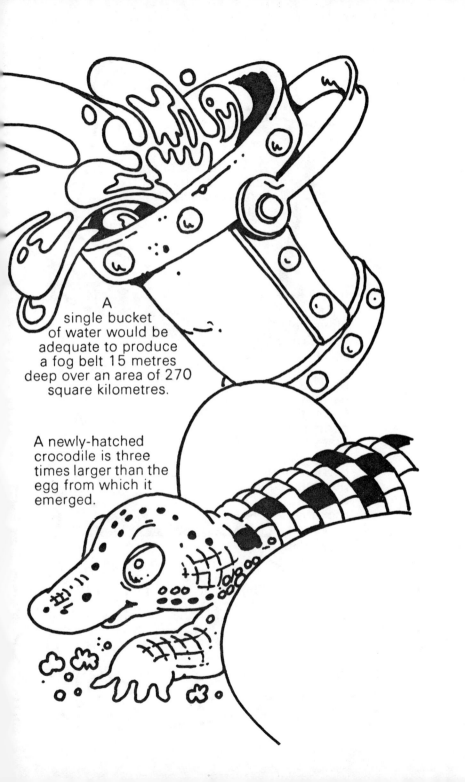

A single bucket of water would be adequate to produce a fog belt 15 metres deep over an area of 270 square kilometres.

A newly-hatched crocodile is three times larger than the egg from which it emerged.

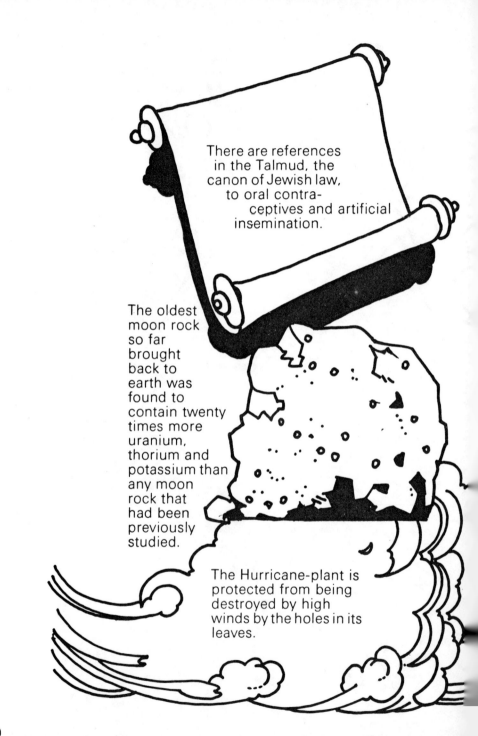

There are references in the Talmud, the canon of Jewish law, to oral contraceptives and artificial insemination.

The oldest moon rock so far brought back to earth was found to contain twenty times more uranium, thorium and potassium than any moon rock that had been previously studied.

The Hurricane-plant is protected from being destroyed by high winds by the holes in its leaves.

Luminous bacteria, that have the ability to give off light, have been cooled to a temperature of –190°C and found to be alive when they were warmed up.

In Jamaica there are some oysters that live in trees.

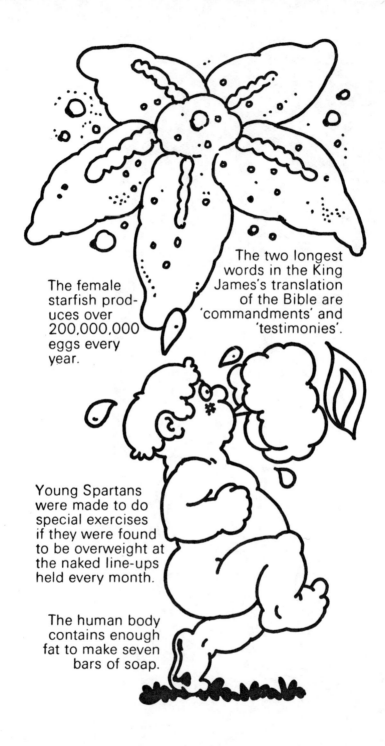

The female starfish produces over 200,000,000 eggs every year.

The two longest words in the King James's translation of the Bible are 'commandments' and 'testimonies'.

Young Spartans were made to do special exercises if they were found to be overweight at the naked line-ups held every month.

The human body contains enough fat to make seven bars of soap.

The Belgian hare is a rabbit.

Petrol and paraffin extinguish fires in bales of cotton more efficiently than water.

Grasshoppers have white blood.

Jane Austen's novel 'Pride and Prejudice' was originally titled 'First Impressions'.

If you wanted to break off your engagement in medieval England you sent your betrothed a sprig of lilac.

Christian Heinrich of Lübeck was able to talk when he was eight weeks old and he knew pieces from the Pentateuch and the Bible at the age of thirteen months.

The water-jets that are used in the manufacture of high carbon steel are strong enough to blast a hole through a pine plank.

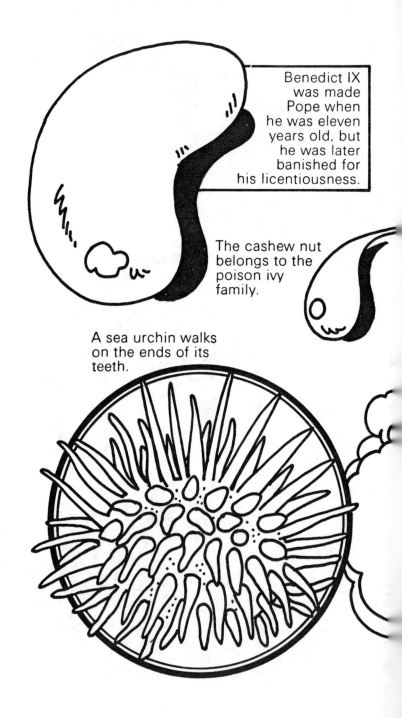

Benedict IX was made Pope when he was eleven years old, but he was later banished for his licentiousness.

The cashew nut belongs to the poison ivy family.

A sea urchin walks on the ends of its teeth.

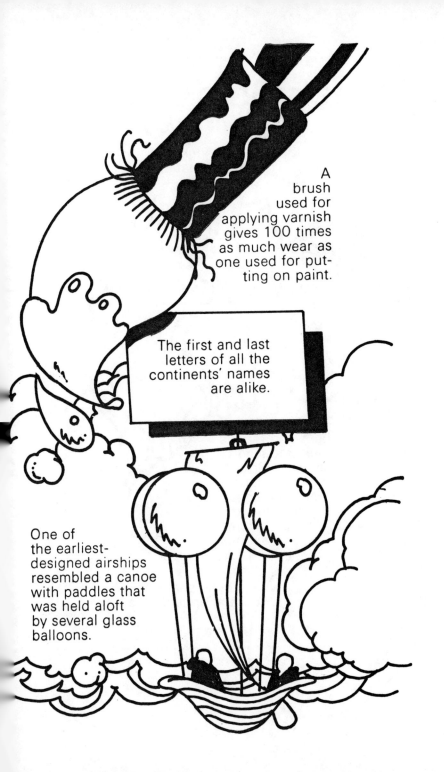

A brush used for applying varnish gives 100 times as much wear as one used for putting on paint.

The first and last letters of all the continents' names are alike.

One of the earliest-designed airships resembled a canoe with paddles that was held aloft by several glass balloons.

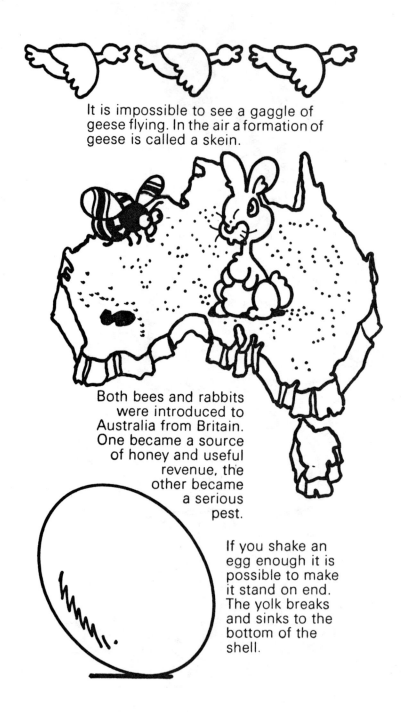

It is impossible to see a gaggle of geese flying. In the air a formation of geese is called a skein.

Both bees and rabbits were introduced to Australia from Britain. One became a source of honey and useful revenue, the other became a serious pest.

If you shake an egg enough it is possible to make it stand on end. The yolk breaks and sinks to the bottom of the shell.

John Keats worked as a dresser in Guy's Hospital, London.

Between 1968 and 1978 Bill Stephenson climbed the Tower in the Palace of Westminster over 2,800 times, which was the same as scaling Mount Everest over seventeen times.

Viscountess Astor, who was the first woman to take her seat in the British House of Commons, was born an American.

The collective noun for barrage
balloon is balloon barrage.

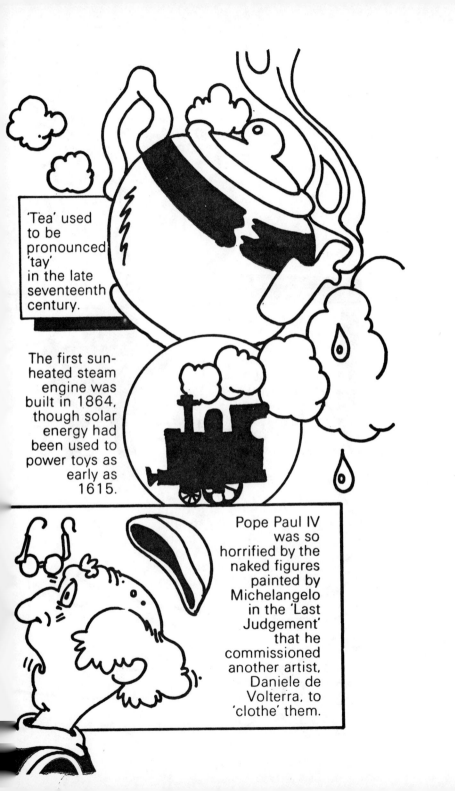

'Tea' used to be pronounced 'tay' in the late seventeenth century.

The first sun-heated steam engine was built in 1864, though solar energy had been used to power toys as early as 1615.

Pope Paul IV was so horrified by the naked figures painted by Michelangelo in the 'Last Judgement' that he commissioned another artist, Daniele de Volterra, to 'clothe' them.

Madame de Pompadour was the first person to own a pet goldfish in France.

The presence of blue blood indicates one of the following conditions: that you are being asphyxiated or you are a lobster.

The Oscars awarded by the American Academy of Motion Picture Arts and Sciences during the Second World War were made out of wood to conserve metal.

Surveys conducted among academics have shown that professors who smoke are twice as likely to write books as those who do not.

The Great White Shark is the only creature living in the sea that has no natural enemies – even killer whales avoid it.

The queen's face which appears on English playing cards was originally that of Elizabeth of York, the wife of Henry VII who was queen of England when playing cards first became popular.

In 1726 Charles Sanson inherited the post of Chief Executioner of Paris from his father. He was seven years old at the time.

The sword-bill humming-bird has a bill that is longer than its body.

The German physicist Professor Philipp Lenard had a morbid fear of the name of Sir Isaac Newton.

The first recorded use of 'dwindle', 'hurry' and 'lonely' were made by Shakespeare.

Benjamin Franklin was the youngest son of a youngest son of a youngest son of a youngest son.

A Neapolitan citizen called Giuseppe de Mai was born with two hearts.

A famous Norwegian cross-country runner Mensen Ernst ran from Paris to Moscow in a fortnight. Swimming 13 large rivers he still managed to average 200 kilometres a day.

If it was possible for the human voice to be carried naturally for great distances through the air, it would take fourteen hours for a shout bellowed in Australia to be heard on the west coast of the USA.

At an altitude of 7,620 metres a pilot can see for a distance of 312 kilometres.

A female mosquito can produce 150,000,000 offspring in one year.

The Portuguese prince, Henry the Navigator, had never navigated a ship in his life and indeed had never left Portugal when he was given the title.

The backbone of a camel is perfectly straight.

Adrienne Cuyot of Belgium was engaged 652 times and married 53 times over a period of 23 years.

According to his contemporaries, Sir Isaac Newton may have been a mathematician of genius, but he was quite incapable of performing any simple mental arithmatic.

Haj Ahmel, who was once Bey of Algeria, had 385 wives who all came from different parts of the world so that none of them could communicate.

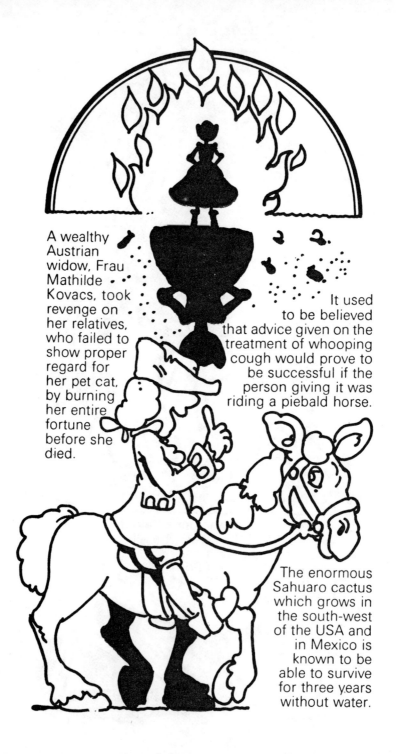

A wealthy Austrian widow, Frau Mathilde Kovacs, took revenge on her relatives, who failed to show proper regard for her pet cat, by burning her entire fortune before she died.

It used to be believed that advice given on the treatment of whooping cough would prove to be successful if the person giving it was riding a piebald horse.

The enormous Sahuaro cactus which grows in the south-west of the USA and in Mexico is known to be able to survive for three years without water.

Erasmus stated
that any man who
failed to catch syphilis
was, in his opinion,
'ignobilis et rusticans',
a base oaf.

Since a frog has no neck it
is neither able to turn its head
nor bend it towards the
ground.

The earliest pictures of Father Christmas, Saint Nicholas, depicted him as a bishop complete with mitre and crook. The jolly old man dressed in red was a creation of 19th century America.

When Mohammed Ali was ruler of Egypt he created two infantry regiments consisting solely of one-eyed soldiers.

Table-tennis was first named 'gossamer'.

The amoeba consumes its food by wrapping its body round it.

Between 1812 and 1813 an American colonel, Russell Farnum, walked from St. Louis to Leningrad.

Otters cause no splash when they plunge into the water.

In 1878 the Queen of Madagascar was buried in a coffin made from 30,000 silver coins riveted together.

The elephant is the only animal with four knees.

Carpet-beetles have lived in corked bottles for two years with nothing to feed on but their own discarded skins.

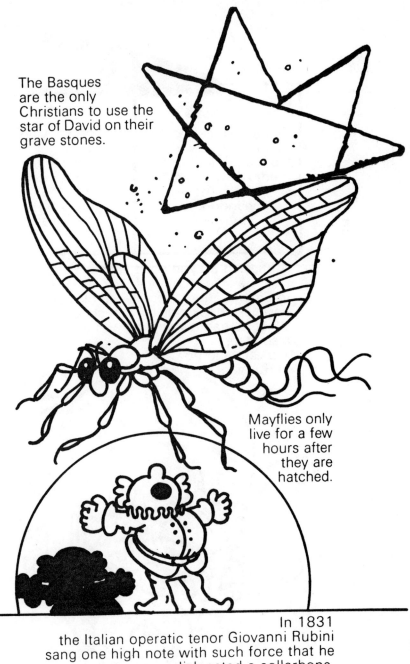

The Basques are the only Christians to use the star of David on their grave stones.

Mayflies only live for a few hours after they are hatched.

In 1831 the Italian operatic tenor Giovanni Rubini sang one high note with such force that he dislocated a collarbone.

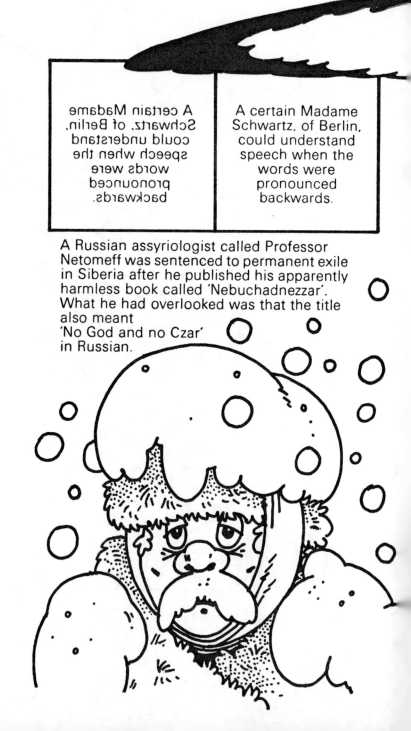

A certain Madame Schwartz, of Berlin, could understand speech when the words were pronounced backwards.

A certain Madame Schwartz, of Berlin, could understand speech when the words were pronounced backwards.

A Russian assyriologist called Professor Netomeff was sentenced to permanent exile in Siberia after he published his apparently harmless book called 'Nebuchadnezzar'. What he had overlooked was that the title also meant 'No God and no Czar' in Russian.

An albatross can fly all day and not flap its wings once.

There is no soda in soda water.

Given that the average person uses a vocabulary of 3,000 words and speaks about 120 words a minute, he would be able to speak his total vocabulary in half an hour.

In Old English the daisy was called 'a daeges eage', 'the eye of the day', because it reminded people of the sun.

In 1660 a duty of four shillings (20 p) was levied on every gallon of coffee made and sold in England.

Surfing is one of the very few aquatic sports in which the participants wear bathing trunks, but try to keep out of the water.

A kiss has been medically described as 'the anatomical juxtaposition of two orbicularis oris muscles in a state of contraction.

Shakespeare mentioned America by name on one occasion in 'The Comedy of Errors' III:2.

The Kiwi lays eggs that sometimes weigh one quarter of its body weight.

The natives of the Solomon Islands used dogs' teeth as currency until this century.

The luckiest number in Italy is 13.

A sixty-five-year-old man has about the same muscular power as a twenty-five-year-old woman.

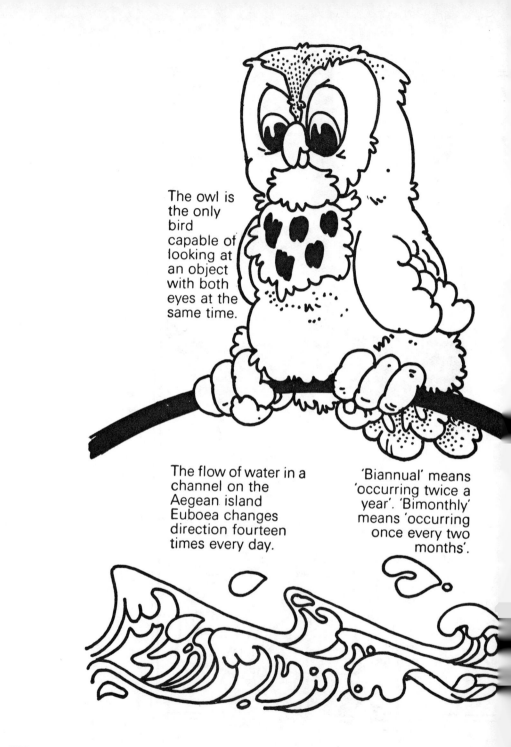

The owl is
the only
bird
capable of
looking at
an object
with both
eyes at the
same time.

The flow of water in a
channel on the
Aegean island
Euboea changes
direction fourteen
times every day.

'Biannual' means
'occurring twice a
year'. 'Bimonthly'
means 'occurring
once every two
months'.

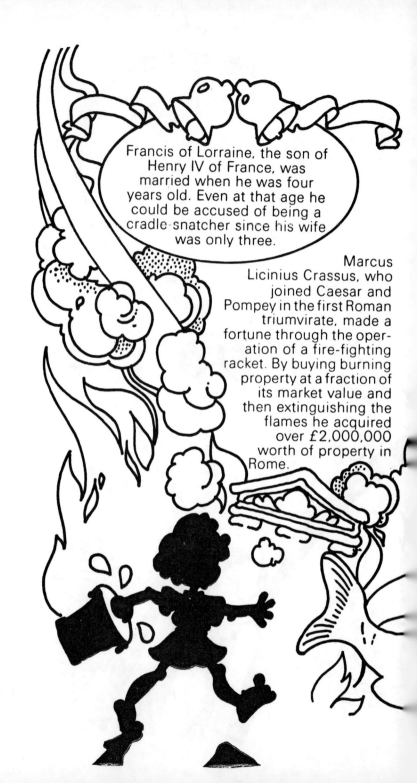

Francis of Lorraine, the son of Henry IV of France, was married when he was four years old. Even at that age he could be accused of being a cradle-snatcher since his wife was only three.

Marcus Licinius Crassus, who joined Caesar and Pompey in the first Roman triumvirate, made a fortune through the operation of a fire-fighting racket. By buying burning property at a fraction of its market value and then extinguishing the flames he acquired over £2,000,000 worth of property in Rome.

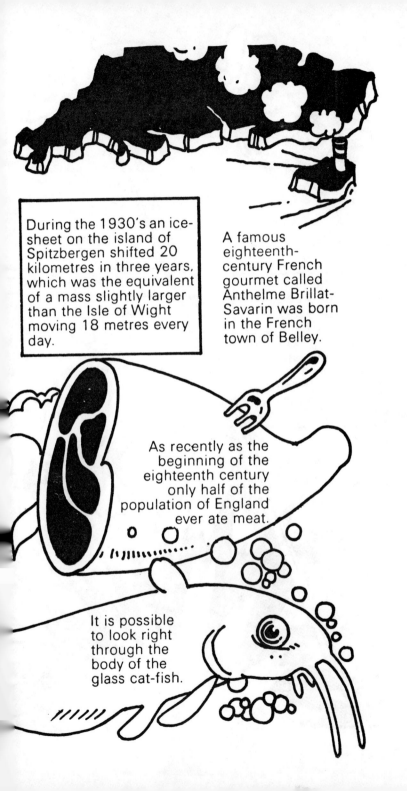

During the 1930's an ice-sheet on the island of Spitzbergen shifted 20 kilometres in three years, which was the equivalent of a mass slightly larger than the Isle of Wight moving 18 metres every day.

A famous eighteenth-century French gourmet called Anthelme Brillat-Savarin was born in the French town of Belley.

As recently as the beginning of the eighteenth century only half of the population of England ever ate meat.

It is possible to look right through the body of the glass cat-fish.

Some of the cells in our body are so small that 200,000 of them could fit onto the head of a pin.

In the two hundred and fifty years between 1564 and 1814 nine Frost Fairs were held on the Thames at Christmas time.

0.47 litres of petrol have the same explosive power as 0.45 kilogrammes of dynamite.

Teddy bears were given their name after the American president Theodore Roosevelt who kept a small bear as a pet.

A German poet called Hans von Thummel was buried in the heart of an oak tree.

There is a flower that grows in Hawaii which opens with a bang. It is called the Firecracker Tree.

The density of Saturn is so low that if the planet fell into a vast sea it would float.

Sunlight does not penetrate more than 400m into the sea.

There are about three and a half times as many countries north of the Equator than south of it.

Mozart composed music while playing billiards, Wagner used to compose wearing fancy dress and most of Rossini's music was composed while the maestro was drunk.

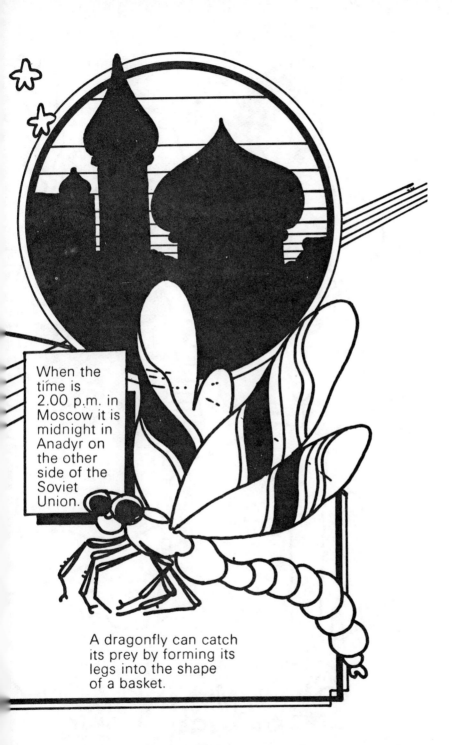

When the time is 2.00 p.m. in Moscow it is midnight in Anadyr on the other side of the Soviet Union.

A dragonfly can catch its prey by forming its legs into the shape of a basket.

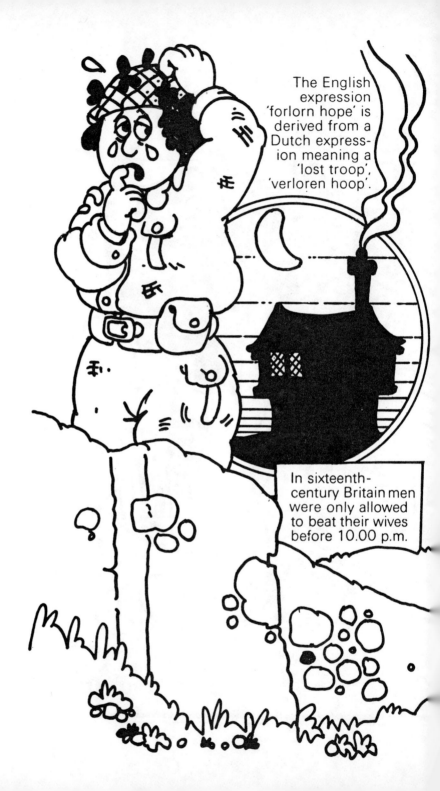

The English expression 'forlorn hope' is derived from a Dutch expression meaning a 'lost troop', 'verloren hoop'.

In sixteenth-century Britain men were only allowed to beat their wives before 10.00 p.m.

Queen Ranavalona of Madagascar prohibited her subjects from appearing in her dreams, under pain of death.

The three-toed sloth partially disguises itself by allowing its body to be covered by a layer of tiny plants.

The Great Wall of China is one of the very few man-made objects that would be visible from the moon.

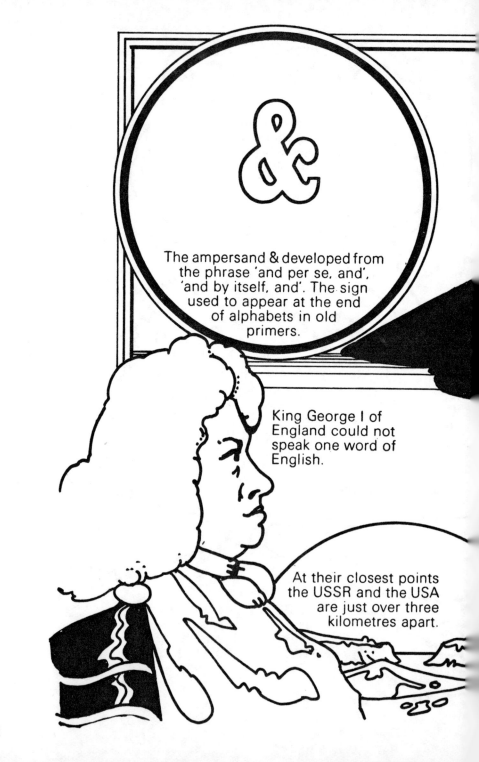

The ampersand & developed from the phrase 'and per se, and', 'and by itself, and'. The sign used to appear at the end of alphabets in old primers.

King George I of England could not speak one word of English.

At their closest points the USSR and the USA are just over three kilometres apart.

The great nineteenth-century actress Sarah Bernhardt played the part of Juliet at the age of seventy.

The American naval hero John Paul Jones ended his career commanding the Russian navy of Catherine the Great.

If all the power from a large bolt of lightning could be harnessed it would provide enough energy to raise an ocean liner two metres into the air.

The opposite sides of a die always add up to seven.

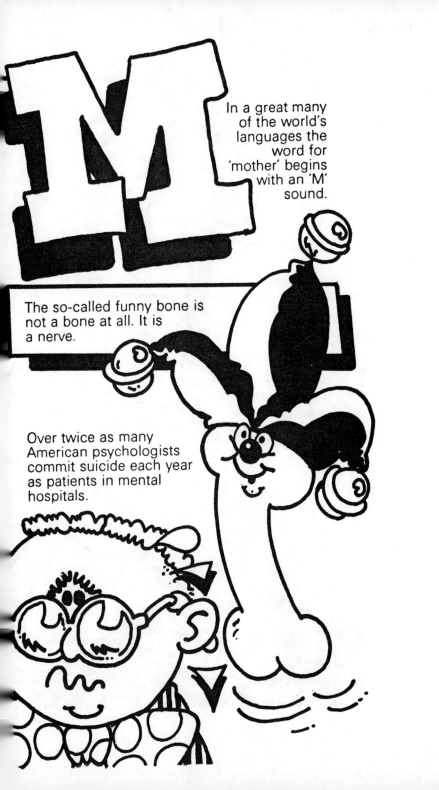

In a great many of the world's languages the word for 'mother' begins with an 'M' sound.

The so-called funny bone is not a bone at all. It is a nerve.

Over twice as many American psychologists commit suicide each year as patients in mental hospitals.

Bonnie
Prince
Charlie
ended his
days as a
drunkard in
Rome.

Handel wrote
many of his
operas with parts
for castrati. The
shortage of
eunuchs today
means that these
works are seldom
performed.

Buddhist burials
can take a long time.
Gravediggers are required
to dig slowly and with
great care to avoid
injuring even
a worm.

Compared with a sparrow, man has a relatively small brain. Whereas a sparrow's brain constitutes about 4.2 per cent of its total body weight, man's brain only takes up 2.5 per cent of his body weight.

One of the witches hung at Salem was found guilty of bewitching a roast pig, a horse and a canoe.

Between 1933 and 1945 Adolf Hitler received a royalty for every postage stamp printed in Germany, because they all bore his photograph.

Cattle can be identified by their nose-prints just as men can be identified by their finger-prints.

There is no army in the Central American state of Costa Rica.

Following the reported landing of a UFO in the US state of Kansas in 1977 the calcium content of the 'landing site' was ten times greater than normal, with the result that nothing could grow on the spot.

If man could jump the same height as a flea in relation to its body-length, anyone walking up Ludgate Hill would be able to jump over St. Paul's Cathedral and think nothing of it.

Originally butterflies were called 'flutterbies'.

To anyone who had the misfortune to be standing on the surface of Pluto, the sun would appear no brighter than Venus appears in the evening sky over the earth.

Within two hours of standing in daylight a bottle of milk loses between half and two thirds of its vitamin B content.

Leading theologians have calculated that when Satan fell from Heaven he was accompanied by exactly 133,306,668 fallen angels.

George Washington often carried a portable sundial to tell him the time instead of a watch.

Noel Coward wrote his famous play 'Private Lives' in a fortnight.

The dormouse spends half the year hibernating.

The only British monarch to have been born in a private house, with a street number, was our present queen, Elizabeth II.

The English word 'poppycock', a very mild way of describing something as 'nonsense', comes from a Dutch word 'papekak' which means 'soft dung'.

Studies into cannibalism have revealed that a man weighing 68 kilos would provide enough meat to feed 75 people at dinner.

The 4th Earl of Salisbury, who was the first European to use cannon in battle in 1428, was also the first soldier to be killed by a cannon in a European battle.

One of the leading American authorities on medical ethics once lectured an audience in Limerick on the harmful effects that uncontrolled sex had on the quality of human life. In a sense he was preaching to the converted - the audience consisted of a hundred nuns.

The Soviet Union is a good place for bachelors looking for pro- spective wives, because for every 100 women there are only 85 men to go round.

374

The hairs of a man's beard are about as strong as copper wires of the same dimensions.

Some anthropologists have suggested that the rhyme used to select individuals in children's games, 'Eeny, meeny, miny, mo', might have derived from early pagan chants for choosing victims for human sacrifices.

What we call Indian ink actually comes from China.

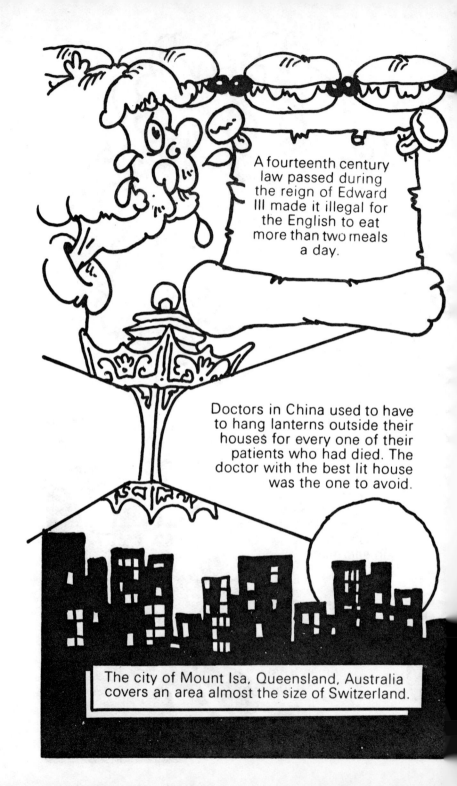

A fourteenth century law passed during the reign of Edward III made it illegal for the English to eat more than two meals a day.

Doctors in China used to have to hang lanterns outside their houses for every one of their patients who had died. The doctor with the best lit house was the one to avoid.

The city of Mount Isa, Queensland, Australia covers an area almost the size of Switzerland.

If all the hot dogs made in the USA every year were joined together, they would stretch from the earth to the moon 2½ times.

Wine is not the only drink that is tested by professional tasters - professional tea tasters are equally busy checking the quality of tea.

A thick glass is more likely to crack if hot water is poured into it than a thin one.

377

The American millionaire Paul Getty once wrote a book entitled 'How To Be Rich'.

Casualty figures indicate that fewer people are killed in flying accidents than the number kicked to death by donkeys.

At one stage, Mohammed, the founder of Islam and revered by every Arab on earth, referred to himself as a 'Jewish' prophet.

A 10-gallon hat in fact barely holds 6 pints (3.4 litres).

The great Roman general Julius Caesar was so conscious of his baldness that he always wore a laurel wreath to disguise the fact.

379

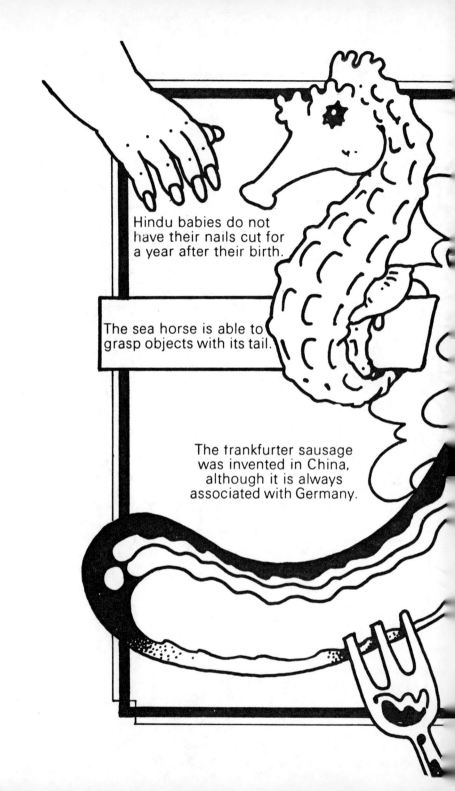

Hindu babies do not
have their nails cut for
a year after their birth.

The sea horse is able to
grasp objects with its tail.

The frankfurter sausage
was invented in China,
although it is always
associated with Germany.

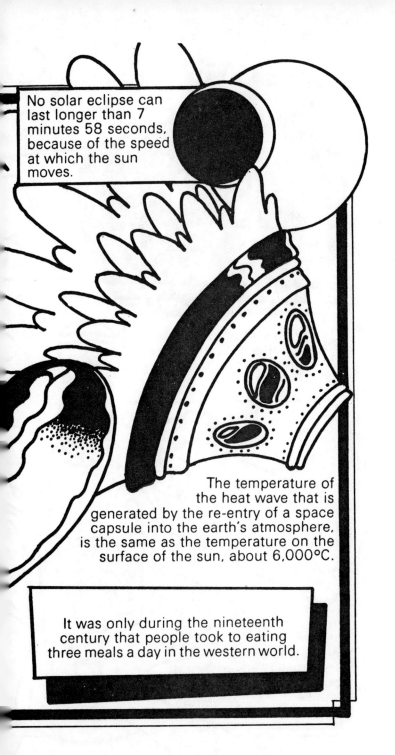

No solar eclipse can last longer than 7 minutes 58 seconds, because of the speed at which the sun moves.

The temperature of the heat wave that is generated by the re-entry of a space capsule into the earth's atmosphere, is the same as the temperature on the surface of the sun, about 6,000°C.

It was only during the nineteenth century that people took to eating three meals a day in the western world.

From the bottom of a deep well it is possible to see the stars during the daytime.

Much of the barley used to make Scottish whisky is imported from North America, Africa and even India.

In its normal state natural gas is odourless. The smell is added by gas companies so that leaks can be detected and accidents prevented.

When a female fish sees a male fish in her aquarium blowing bubbles it means he is ready for breeding.

In the Bible the Red Sea is never referred to by name.

Swedish girls who want to get an idea of their future husbands put seven different flowers under their pillows on Midsummer's night. Tradition holds that they will then dream about the lucky man.

Dentists extract about four tons of rotten teeth every year from the mouths of children in England and Wales.

In ancient Greece dice used to be made from the ankle-bones of sheep.

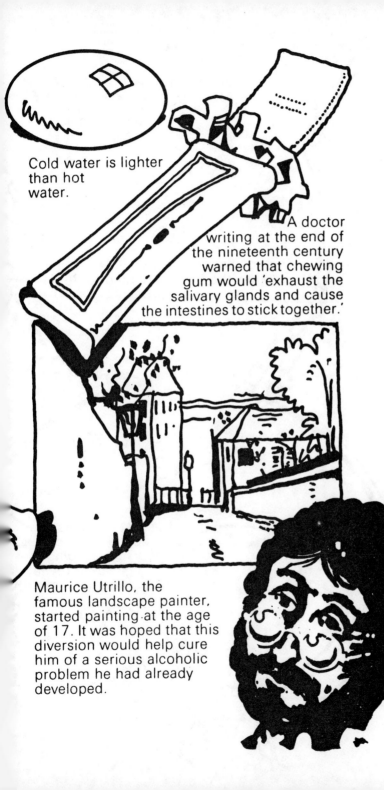

Cold water is lighter than hot water.

A doctor writing at the end of the nineteenth century warned that chewing gum would 'exhaust the salivary glands and cause the intestines to stick together.'

Maurice Utrillo, the famous landscape painter, started painting at the age of 17. It was hoped that this diversion would help cure him of a serious alcoholic problem he had already developed.

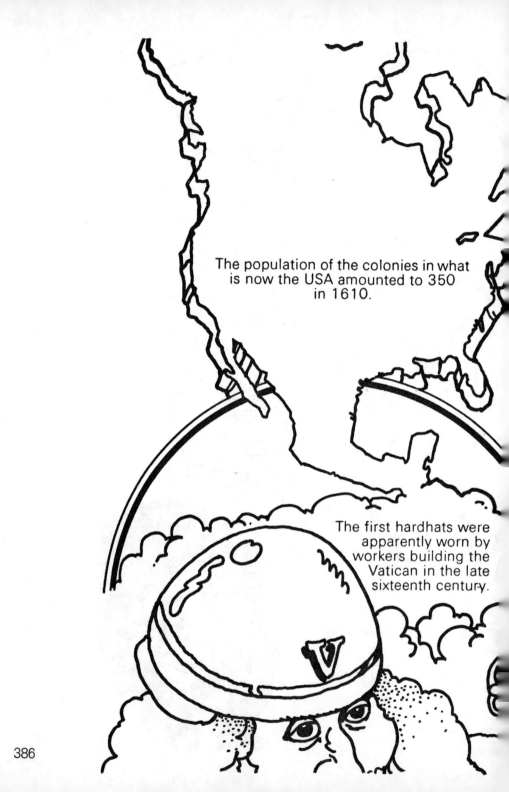

The population of the colonies in what is now the USA amounted to 350 in 1610.

The first hardhats were apparently worn by workers building the Vatican in the late sixteenth century.

The volume of Lake Ontario, in North America, is 4,500 times greater than the volume of Lake Windermere, the largest lake in England.

Young men of the Loango and other African tribes are forbidden to speak to girls unless the girls' mothers are present.

160 cars could drive side by side on the world's widest road, the Monumental Axis in Brazil.

Amongst the Arabs
there are nearly
1,000 different
words for
a camel.

The distance between the earth and the sun is about 385 times the distance between the earth and the moon.

No point in Britain is more than 120 km from the sea

Zoologists estimate that between twelve and sixteen times more animal species have died out during the last four hundred years than would have become extinct if modern man had never lived.

The only bird that has its nostrils at the end of its bill is the kiwi.

As much heat is required to melt a kilo of snow as is needed to boil a litre of soup at room temperature.

The most widely eaten green vegetable in the world is the lettuce.

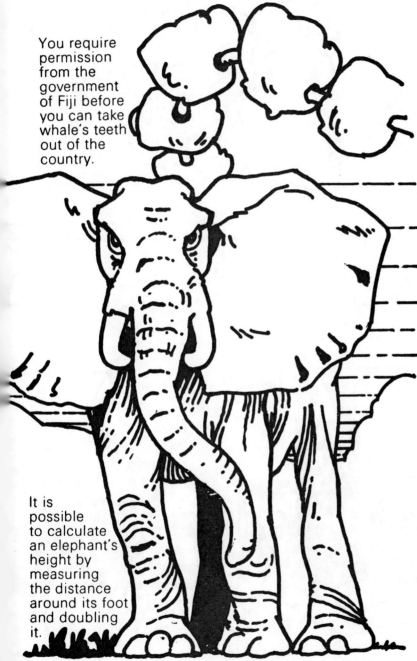

You require permission from the government of Fiji before you can take whale's teeth out of the country.

It is possible to calculate an elephant's height by measuring the distance around its foot and doubling it.

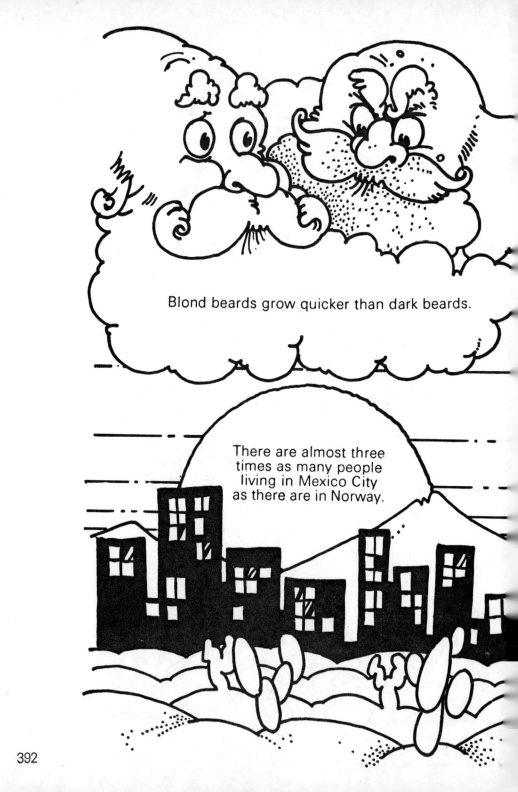

Blond beards grow quicker than dark beards.

There are almost three times as many people living in Mexico City as there are in Norway.

Before becoming an idol of the cinema screen Greta Garbo worked as a manicurist in a Stockholm barbershop.

Robert E. Lee is probably the only general who has been offered the command of both opposing forces in any war.

The female black widow
spider eats her partner
after mating, hence her
name. Some females
manage to get through
twenty-five husbands in
a day in this
manner.

Kaleidoscopes
were originally
intended to
help textile
designers,
when they
were
invented
in
1816.

One of the best natural lubricants in the world is castor oil. Even jet aircraft have a dose now and then to keep them running smoothly.

Among many Irish cures that strike the sceptical mind as being of doubtful medical value is one for mumps that requires the patient to be led by reins round a pigsty three times.

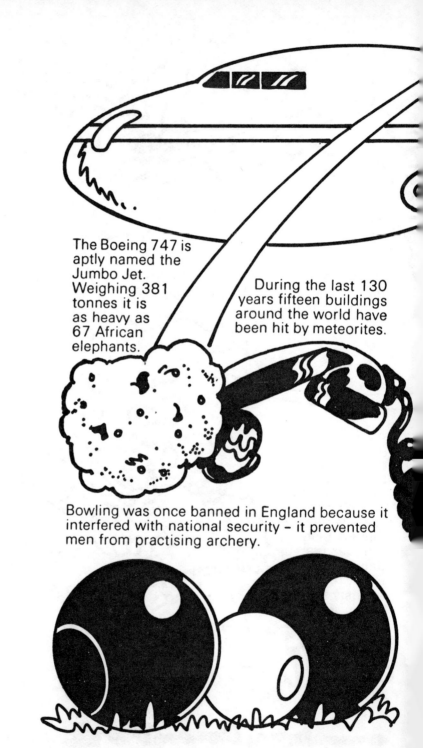

The Boeing 747 is aptly named the Jumbo Jet. Weighing 381 tonnes it is as heavy as 67 African elephants.

During the last 130 years fifteen buildings around the world have been hit by meteorites.

Bowling was once banned in England because it interfered with national security – it prevented men from practising archery.

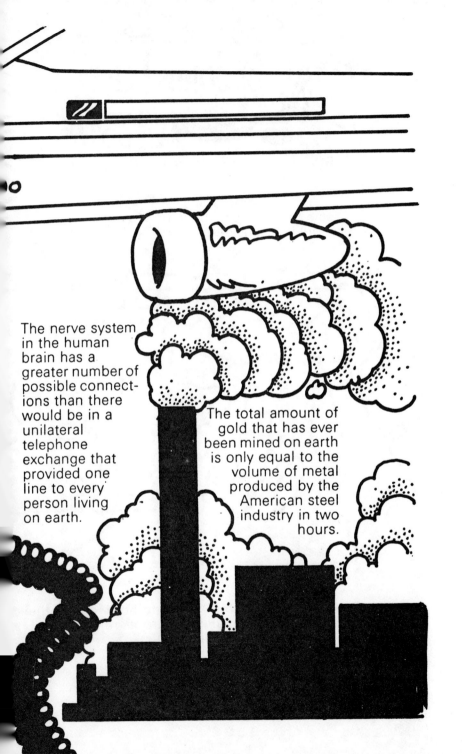

The nerve system in the human brain has a greater number of possible connections than there would be in a unilateral telephone exchange that provided one line to every person living on earth.

The total amount of gold that has ever been mined on earth is only equal to the volume of metal produced by the American steel industry in two hours.

St. John's Lane

St. John's Lane in Rome is just 48cm wide.

According to many scientists the Chihuahua should be considered as a type of rodent and not as a dog at all.

The first man to climb the Matterhorn, one of the most difficult mountains in Europe, rejoiced in the name of Mr. Whymper.

In 1971 the world's poorest people were discovered living in caves in the central Philippines. They had no domestic animals, no farming, no clothes and they lived without the wheel or pottery.

In Siberia milk is often sold frozen on a stick, like a large ice-lolly, as a convenient way of carrying it about.

It is estimated that the Tour de France costs the French economy over £1,000,000,000 in lost production during the three week fervour with which it grips the country.

The last trial in which an animal was condemned to death took place in France in 1740. A cow was found guilty of sorcery and was hanged on the gallows.

In the summer of 1977 Emma Disley climbed up Mount Snowdon on a pair of stilts to raise funds for an animal charity.

In their early years in Europe potatoes had a hard time. They were blamed for epidemics of leprosy and syphilis and many people believed that eating potatoes was a certain way of shortening your life.

The human mouth contains more bacteria than any other orifice in the body.

Taiwan is the largest exporter of mushrooms in the world.

More UFO's are sighted at those times when Mars is near the earth than at any other times.

Heat is better retained in moist air than in dry air, which is why tropical nights are warm and desert nights cold.

Originally Eau de Cologne was developed as a means of protection against the plague.

A law was passed in England during the reign of Elizabeth I that required men with beards to pay a special tax.

Snails only mate once in their lifetime. However, the act often lasts for as long as twelve hours.

Left-handed German troops were provided with specially designed weapons during the Second World War.

Roman medicine advocated the drinking of fresh gladiator blood as one of the possible cures for epilepsy.

The longest stroke of lightning that has ever been measured stretched for 32 km. across the sky.

It is virtually impossible for human skin to be completely black.

26 countries in the world have no coastline at all.

An owl is able
to turn its
head in a
complete
circle.

London was the first city in the
world to have a population that
exceeded one million. This figure
was passed at the turn of the 19th
century.

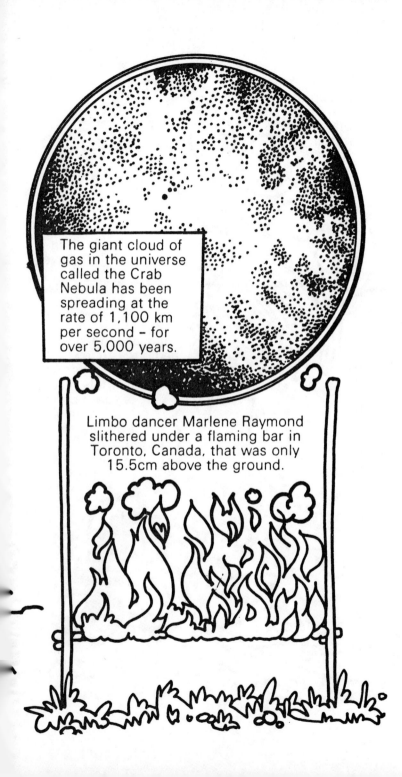

The giant cloud of gas in the universe called the Crab Nebula has been spreading at the rate of 1,100 km per second – for over 5,000 years.

Limbo dancer Marlene Raymond slithered under a flaming bar in Toronto, Canada, that was only 15.5cm above the ground.

Jupiter is large enough to contain all the other planets in the solar system.

The people of ancient Carthage attempted to relieve attacks of indigestion by rubbing a cow's tail on their abdomens.

If ever food stocks begin to run low it is worth remembering that whale meat is very rich in Vitamin C. Unfortunately whales are rather scarce as well.

Pure gold is so soft that it can be moulded in the hands.

In New York it is against the law to leave a shop dummy standing naked in a shop window.

409

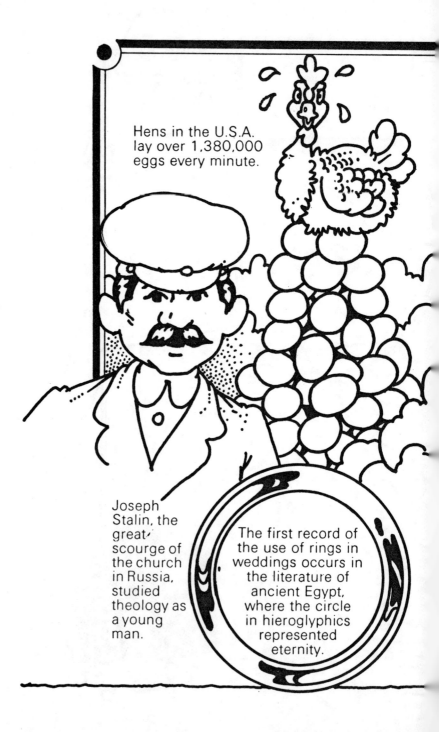

Hens in the U.S.A. lay over 1,380,000 eggs every minute.

Joseph Stalin, the great scourge of the church in Russia, studied theology as a young man.

The first record of the use of rings in weddings occurs in the literature of ancient Egypt, where the circle in hieroglyphics represented eternity.

The leading cereal company in North America, The Quaker Oats Company, actually sells more pet food than cereal.

The Colosseum in Rome must rank as one of the longest running centres of entertainment in the world. It opened in A.D. 80 and shows were staged there for the next 400 years.

Bubbles are round because the air enclosed inside them presses equally on all parts, making every surface the same distance from its centre.

The Lutine Bell which hangs in the Under-writing Room at Lloyds is struck to announce items of news. When the bell is struck once it indicates that bad news will be announced. When it is struck twice good news follows.

It takes the light from Pluto six hours to reach earth.

A car moving at 88km/h will travel over 17 metres in the time it takes the driver to move his foot from the accelerator to the brake.

The first cooking demonstration broadcast on television showed the viewers how to make an omelette.

Industrial disputes occurred in the ancient world as well. In 1160 B.C. workmen building the tomb of the Egyptian Pharaoh Rameses III went on strike in support of a pay claim designed to keep pace with the rise in the cost of living.

FAIR DEAL!

The best known English writer William Shakespeare and the best known Spanish writer Miguel de Cervantes, died on the same day, 23 April, 1616.

The only animal that cries is man.

Jayne Mansfield had the same bust measurement as Marie Antoinette.

President John F. Kennedy used to read four newspapers in twenty minutes.

Queen Victoria's rat catcher received a higher salary in 1857 than the poet laureate, Alfred Lord Tennyson.

Clean snow melts slower than snow which is dirty.

96 per cent of babies arrive at times different from those predicted by the medical profession.

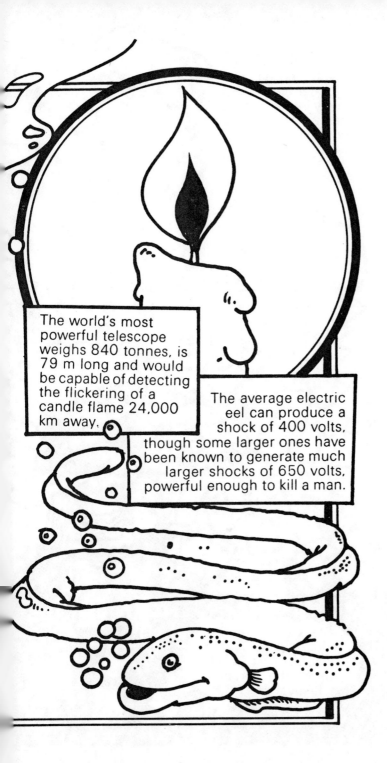

The world's most powerful telescope weighs 840 tonnes, is 79 m long and would be capable of detecting the flickering of a candle flame 24,000 km away.

The average electric eel can produce a shock of 400 volts, though some larger ones have been known to generate much larger shocks of 650 volts, powerful enough to kill a man.

If you smoke twenty high-tar cigarettes every day you inhale half a cup full of tar each year.

The lowest valued note in the world is the Hong Kong 1 cent note, of which 1,200 equal £1.00.

Black snow fell over more than 18,000 km² of south-east Sweden during the Christmas festival of 1969.

Based on estimates that the library of Yale University, U.S.A. doubles in size every sixteen years, it has been calculated that by the year 2,000 the library will house a total of 200,000,000 volumes that would stretch from the North Pole to the Equator.

In the English language 99 per cent of what people say is accounted for by a mere 2,000 words and 25 per cent by only 10 words.

One sixth of the land on earth
is in the Soviet Union.

The U.S. mint once
made the dreadful
mistake of stamping the phrase 'In Gold We Trust'
on a batch of gold coins. The motto should of
course read 'In God We Trust'.

Josef Stalin smoked his pipe in public. In private he chain-smoked cigarettes.

The last mules employed in a British army transport corps were de-mobbed in 1975.

If you were born in the first three months of the year you are more likely to be a schizophrenic or a manic depressive than those born later

The Panama
Canal is the only
place on earth
where you can
watch the sun rise
over the Pacific
and set in the
Atlantic. This is
due to the bend
in the isthmus
through which
the canal was
cut.

Tin cans are
over 97 per
cent steel.

Chewing
gum
while
peeling
onions
prevents
you from
crying.

Amongst the debris scattered over the moon's surface by American astronauts are the golf balls driven by Alan Shepard in 1971. Even though he was only using a six iron and despite his bulky space-suit he was still able to hit the balls 365 metres in the low gravity environment.

The night that the United Nations voted in favour of establishing Israel the Dead Sea Scrolls were deciphered for the first time.

Spell 'evil' backwards and you get the word 'live'.

The stones from the Great Pyramid at Cheops could be used to build a wall three metres high all the way round France.

The practice of castrating choristers in the Vatican was only discontinued by a ruling of Pope Leo XIII less than 100 years ago.

If sugar is added to a glass of water and an egg is then added, the egg will float in the water.

During the eighteenth century many large country mansions burnt over one ton of coal each day. At Compton Wynyates one ton of coal was consumed in the kitchen alone every day.

Christianity has the largest number of followers on earth, twice as many as the second largest religion Islam. Amongst Christians, Roman Catholics are more numerous than all the other Christian groups combined.

The seeds of an Arctic Lupin estimated to be 10,000 years old have been successfully germinated and grown in a laboratory experiment.

Extensive studies into the problem have revealed that men are twice as likely to fall out of hospital beds as women.

In the Dominican Republic you can obtain a divorce in one day.

Cats cannot taste sweet foods.

During a performance of Benjamin Britten's opera 'Billy Budd' the singer Rhydderch Davies was so engrossed in the aria she stepped off the stage into the orchestra pit. At the time she was singing 'Look Where You Go'.

The Empire State Building in New York city could be fitted eight times into the world's deepest mine which is 3,840m deep.

There is no impartial evidence to indicate that Richard III of England was a hunchback.

One of the injuries which frequently afflicts skiers is Gamekeeper's Thumb.

A common method of committing suicide in ancient China was by eating half a kilo of salt.

Over 140,000 crocuses are needed to make one kilo of saffron.

The study and analysis of blow pipes is called pyritology.

Cockroaches can survive for several weeks after having their heads cut off.

There are 3 kilometres of road in Belgium for every square kilometre of land.

Proportionately the earth's crust is about the same thickness in ratio to its mass as an egg-shell is to an egg.

The surname of the legendary liberator of Switzerland, William Tell, means 'the mad'.

India is the leading film making country in the world. More than twice as many films are made in India each year than in France, the third highest film producer in the world.

The only insect producing food that is eaten by man is the bee.

A temperature change of 27.2°C took place in Spearfish, South Dakota, USA, one morning in 1943, in the space of only two minutes.

Every day a common shrew will eat two-thirds of its own body weight.

If goldfish are left in a dark room for a long period they will frequently turn white.

A seventeenth-century law passed in the New England state of Massachusetts made it illegal to celebrate Christmas.

Glaciers cover about 10 per cent of the earth's land surface or almost the same area as the whole South American continent.

Until 1970 it was against the law to play the drums in the Middle Eastern state of Oman.

In Tibet it is generally regarded as a gesture of respect towards guests if you stick out your tongue at them.

In 1941 an Admiralty boffin dreamt up the idea of building an aircraft carrier out of ice. Work on the project actually began in 1942 and it was only suspended when one major problem proved impossible to overcome – the 'vessel' kept sinking.

Astronomers have estimated that more than 100 million comets revolve around the sun.

Every bucket of sea water contains about two cupfuls of dissolved minerals, which make the sea taste salty.

The rate of acceleration of
the flea that inhabits
human beings is very
nearly thirty times
greater, when it jumps,
than the speed at which a
human being blacks out.

St. Simeon the Younger
spent the last forty-five
years of his life sitting
on top of a pole in Syria.

Fort Worth airport in
Texas covers an area
greater than six and a
half thousand football
pitches. It is the largest
airport in the world.

Russian scientists estimate that
Lake Baskunchak could supply the whole
world with salt for over two thousand years.

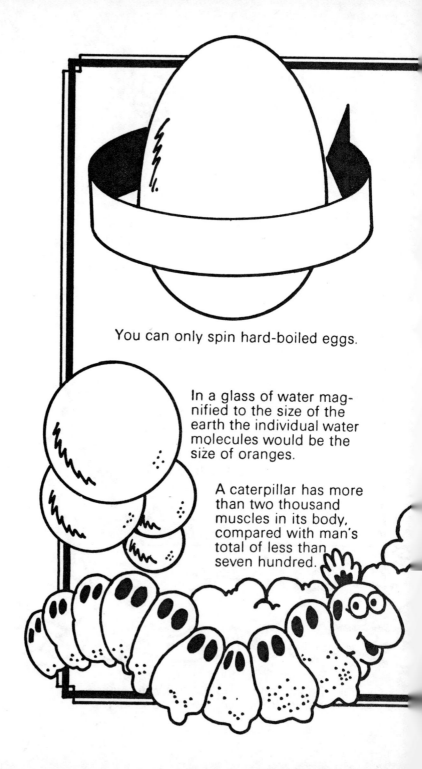

You can only spin hard-boiled eggs.

In a glass of water magnified to the size of the earth the individual water molecules would be the size of oranges.

A caterpillar has more than two thousand muscles in its body, compared with man's total of less than seven hundred.

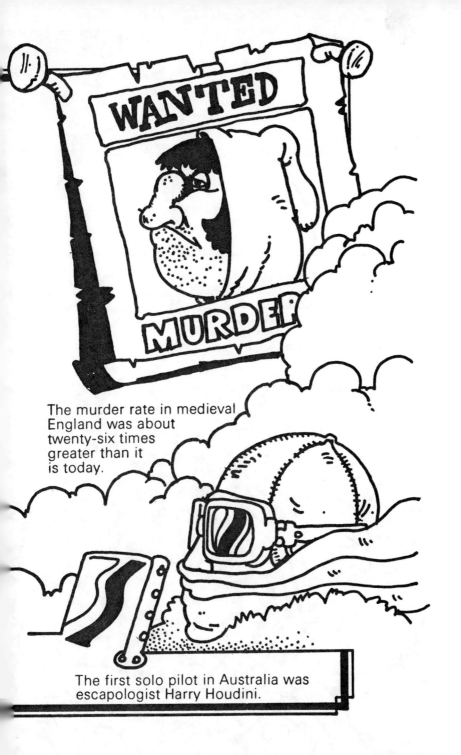

The murder rate in medieval England was about twenty-six times greater than it is today.

The first solo pilot in Australia was escapologist Harry Houdini.

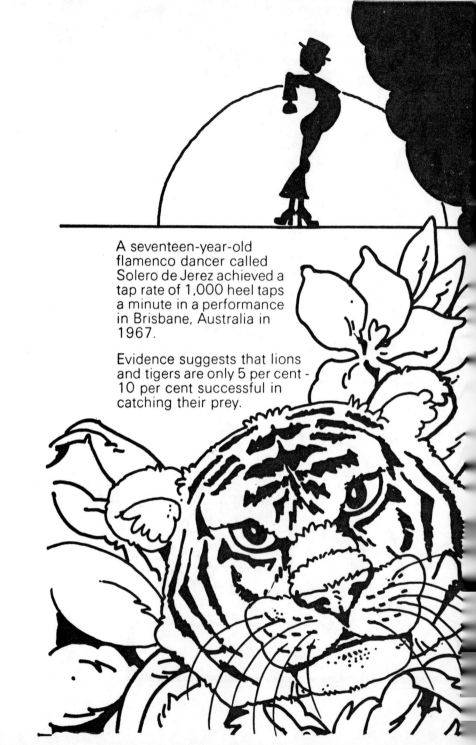

A seventeen-year-old flamenco dancer called Solero de Jerez achieved a tap rate of 1,000 heel taps a minute in a performance in Brisbane, Australia in 1967.

Evidence suggests that lions and tigers are only 5 per cent - 10 per cent successful in catching their prey.

At this very moment there are two thousand thunderstorms taking place somewhere above the earth's surface.

The orchid gets its name from the Greek word for 'testicles', suggesting that at one time the flower may have possessed aphrodisiac qualities.

You need 120 drops of water to fill a teaspoon.

Women's ears were believed to be erogenous zones in the Middle Ages and had to be suitably covered.

Many soldiers in ancient Greece went into battle naked from the waist downwards.

A French-convict, Paul Hubert, had spent twenty-one years of his life sentence in solitary confinement when the case for which he had been convicted was re-examined. It was then discovered that he had been found guilty of murdering himself.

Burning at the stake was still a legal method of execution in many areas of the U.S.A. even until the early 1800's.

Money paid as a ransom to a kidnapper is tax deductable in the U.S.A.

Only a quarter of the American coin called a 'nickel' is actually made from the metal nickel. The rest of the coin is copper.

In Chinese the character for east is written by placing the character for the sun behind that for a tree:

日-sun 木-tree 東-east

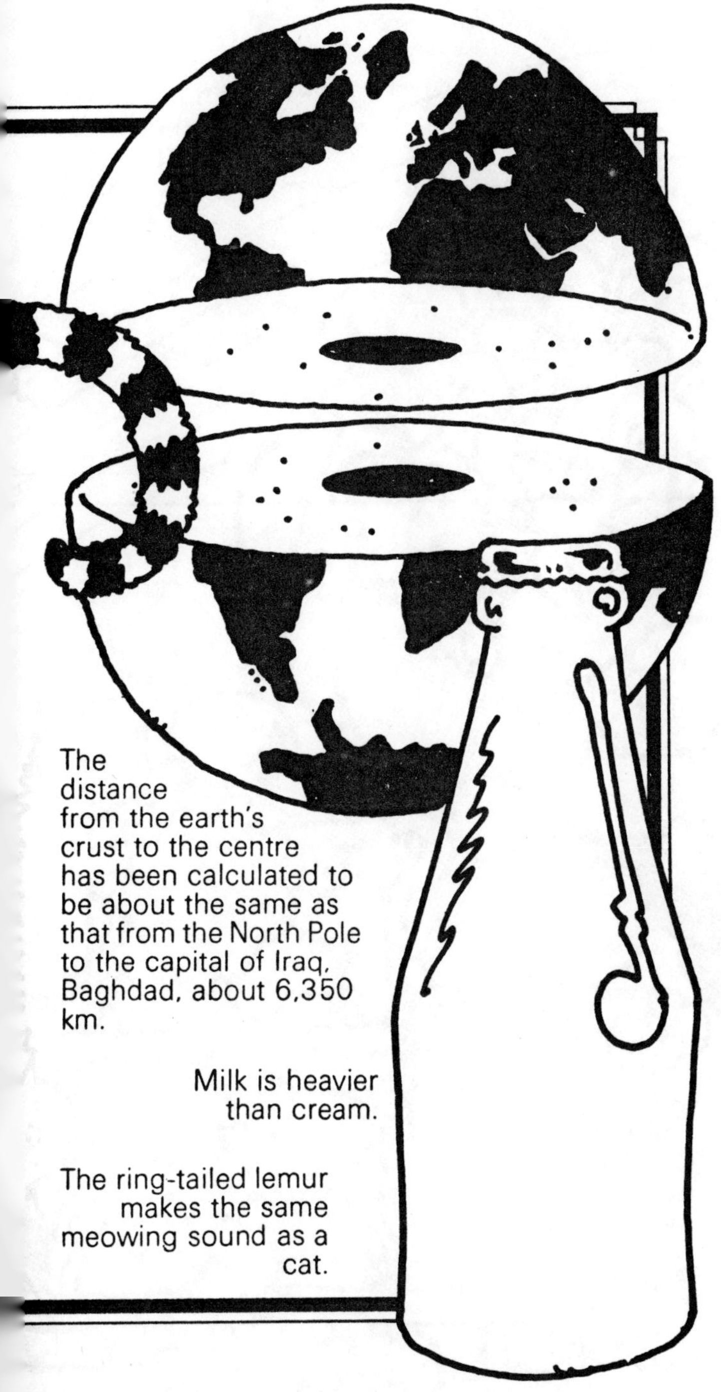

The
distance
from the earth's
crust to the centre
has been calculated to
be about the same as
that from the North Pole
to the capital of Iraq,
Baghdad, about 6,350
km.

Milk is heavier
than cream.

The ring-tailed lemur
makes the same
meowing sound as a
cat.

Rainbows only occur when the sun is at an angle of less than 40° above the horizon.

80 per cent of the rose species on earth come from Asia.

In Germany the annual Oktoberfest is held for a fort-night – most of which falls within September.

For an entire year, Jonathan Swift, the author of 'Gulliver's Travels', refused to speak to anyone.

The altitude limit for birds is roughly the same as the summit of Mount Everest, 8,848m. above sea level.

Medieval Japanese women used to stain their teeth black as a way of improving their beauty.

Our brains are more watery than our blood - they are four fifths water.

Over half the volcanoes that are active today are situated around the shore of the Pacific Ocean.

There are several
nutritional sub-
stances in
tobacco leaves
which could keep
you alive for a
while if there was
no other food to
eat – of course
this tobacco
would have to be
chewed, not
smoked.

If you ever happen
to find yourself pelted
by lice and slugs thrown
by a female inhabitant of
nothern Siberia, this is
only her way of
saying
'I love you'.

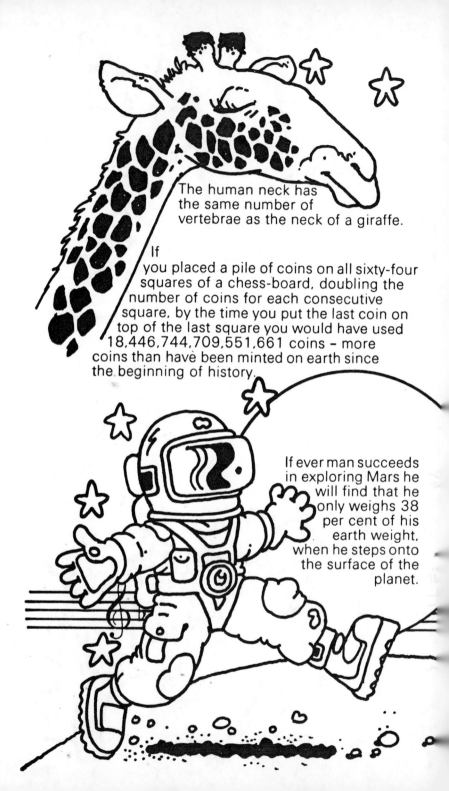

The human neck has the same number of vertebrae as the neck of a giraffe.

If you placed a pile of coins on all sixty-four squares of a chess-board, doubling the number of coins for each consecutive square, by the time you put the last coin on top of the last square you would have used 18,446,744,709,551,661 coins – more coins than have been minted on earth since the beginning of history.

If ever man succeeds in exploring Mars he will find that he only weighs 38 per cent of his earth weight, when he steps onto the surface of the planet.

At night clouds fly
lower than they
do during the day

On one occasion, a cow
was sentenced to two
days in prison after
being convicted
of eating the
lawn outside the
courthouse of
the New Zealand
capital Wellington.

The French composer Darius
Milhaud composed an opera called
'The Deliverance of Theseus'
which lasted seven and
a half minutes.

Until less
than one
hundred
years ago
corpses
awaiting
burial used
to be stored
in the
cellars of
public
houses.

When it
swims a penguin
uses its wings as rudders.

William Huskisson who became the first person to be run over by a railway train is commemorated by a two and a half metre high statue clad in a Roman toga.

We blink about 25 times a minute and each blink lasts for about one fifth of a second.

It was popularly believed in the 16th century that the breath of billy-goats protected the occupants of a house from catching the plague.

St. Luke was the only New Testament writer who was not Jewish.

In America The Rolls Royce Silver Shadow is classified as a 'compact car'.

The Cape Buffalo has killed more hunters than any other wild animal.

In 1348, the year in which the Black Death reached England, it rained almost continually from mid-June until Christmas.

David Garrick,
the leading
18th century
actor, coined a
rather
indecorous
nickname for
William Shakespeare,
'Avonian Willy'.

In Spain Sir Francis Drake
was nicknamed El Draque
(The Dragon) and
Spanish mothers
still use him
as a bogey
man to threaten
their disobed-
ient children.

The three
golden balls
that became the
symbol of pawn-
brokers' shops
originally
appeared on the
coat of arms of
the Medici family,
the most powerful
moneylenders in
Florence.

One of the many attractions of the Astor House hotel which opened in New York City in 1836, was the virtually unique service of running hot water on the first floor.

Holinshed records in his Chronicles that more English knights were killed by lightning during a thunderstorm in 1360 than were killed at the battles of Crécy and Poitiers.

The
insulation
on the fuel tanks
of the Saturn rocket
is so effective that
an ice cube stored
inside would take
eight years to melt.

One
hundred
and
twenty
drops of
water are
needed to
fill a tea-
spoon.

Every hour 180 medical
journals are published
around the world.

Japanese skipping expert, Katsumi Suzuki, can make five turns in one jump.

Hindus cannot be excommunicated from their religion, no matter what they do.

The Greek philosopher Aristotle believed that the most delicate meat to eat was the flesh of camels.

Rome and Madrid
lie almost exactly
due east of
Chicago.

Although lions
are traditionally
depicted as fierce
killers, they leave
their wives to
actually kill 90 per
cent of the prey,
before they
saunter up and
devour the first
portion,
the 'lion's share'.

The last British monarch to
use the royal veto was
Queen Anne, who refused to
give Royal assent to the
Scottish Militia Bill in 1707.

Because water is very scarce in Morocco the wealthy regard it as an important status symbol, displaying their affluence by building enormous fountains in front of their homes.

The doctors treating Henry VIII diagnosed that the King had contracted venereal disease from Cardinal Wolsey who had apparently been rash enough to whisper in his sovereign's ear.

An anagram of 'punishment'
is 'nine thumps'.

The English word 'calculate'
is derived from the Latin word
for a stone, 'calculus'

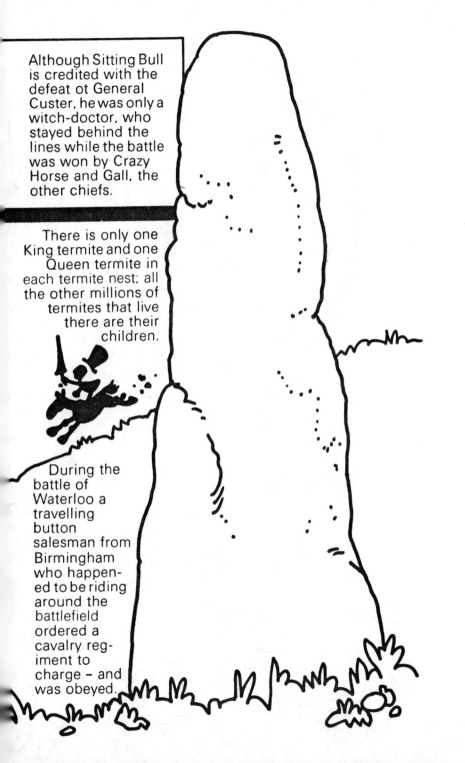

Although Sitting Bull is credited with the defeat ot General Custer, he was only a witch-doctor, who stayed behind the lines while the battle was won by Crazy Horse and Gall, the other chiefs.

There is only one King termite and one Queen termite in each termite nest; all the other millions of termites that live there are their children.

During the battle of Waterloo a travelling button salesman from Birmingham who happened to be riding around the battlefield ordered a cavalry regiment to charge – and was obeyed.

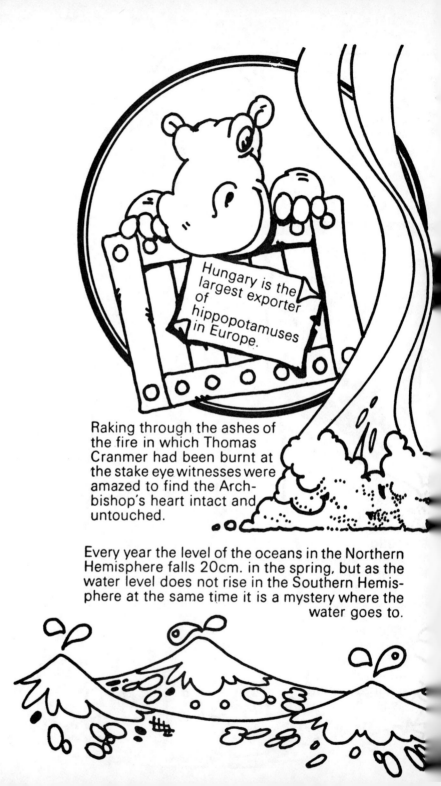

Hungary is the largest exporter of hippopotamuses in Europe.

Raking through the ashes of the fire in which Thomas Cranmer had been burnt at the stake eye witnesses were amazed to find the Archbishop's heart intact and untouched.

Every year the level of the oceans in the Northern Hemisphere falls 20cm. in the spring, but as the water level does not rise in the Southern Hemisphere at the same time it is a mystery where the water goes to.

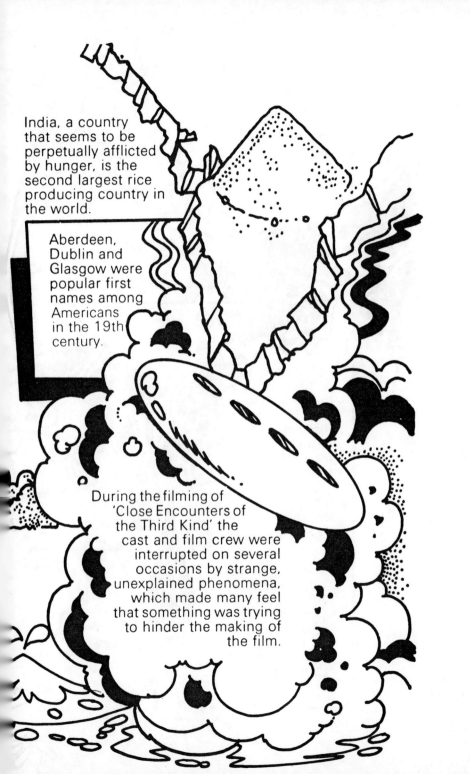

India, a country that seems to be perpetually afflicted by hunger, is the second largest rice producing country in the world.

Aberdeen, Dublin and Glasgow were popular first names among Americans in the 19th century.

During the filming of 'Close Encounters of the Third Kind' the cast and film crew were interrupted on several occasions by strange, unexplained phenomena, which made many feel that something was trying to hinder the making of the film.

465

In the early days of the colony of Virginia, conspiring to damage or destroy a tobacco plant was an offence that carried the death penalty.

Pollution is so bad in the Sargasso Sea that there is more oil on the surface than the sea-weed that gives the sea its name.

The only English pope, Nicholas Breakspear (Adrian IV), died choking over a fly he had swallowed while drinking.

If all the stars in the Milky Way had names, anyone trying to say their names one after the other would take 4,000 years, even if they could say one name every second without ever stopping.

It is possible to read by the light produced by half a dozen large fire flies.

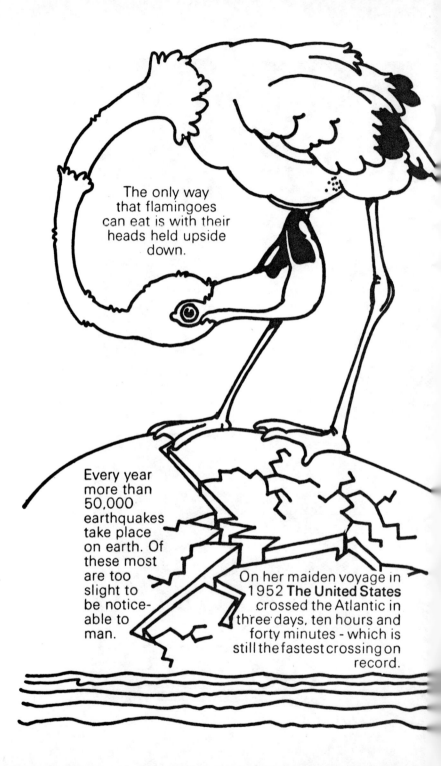

The only way that flamingoes can eat is with their heads held upside down.

Every year more than 50,000 earthquakes take place on earth. Of these most are too slight to be notice-able to man.

On her maiden voyage in 1952 **The United States** crossed the Atlantic in three days, ten hours and forty minutes - which is still the fastest crossing on record.

Anyone called Jane who has ideas of becoming a queen should think very carefully. All other queens named Jane have either died young, gone mad, been dethroned, been imprisoned or been murdered.

Diamonds were more commonly worn by men than women until the fifteenth century.

A sharp cough may well move air inside the body faster than the speed of sound.

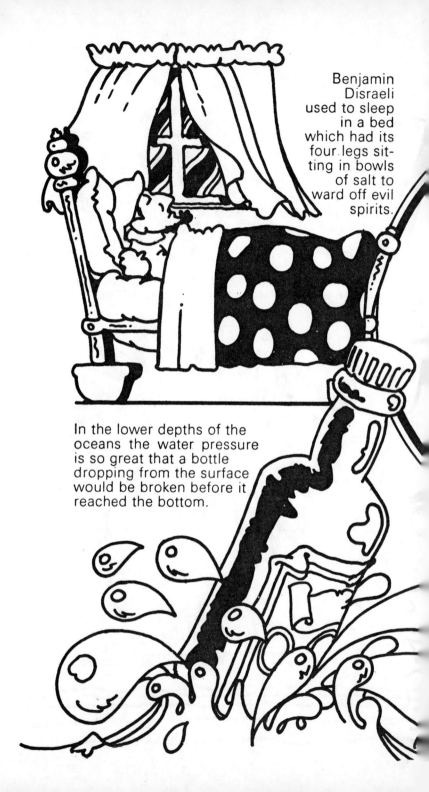

Benjamin Disraeli used to sleep in a bed which had its four legs sitting in bowls of salt to ward off evil spirits.

In the lower depths of the oceans the water pressure is so great that a bottle dropping from the surface would be broken before it reached the bottom.

The ancient Greeks believed that there were two compartments in the womb. Girls came from the left and boys from the right.

Swami Maujgiri Maharij performed his penance in an unusual way to western observers. He stood continuously for seventeen years and even when he went to sleep he was held upright by a board.

When giraffes press their necks against each other they are expressing mutual affection.

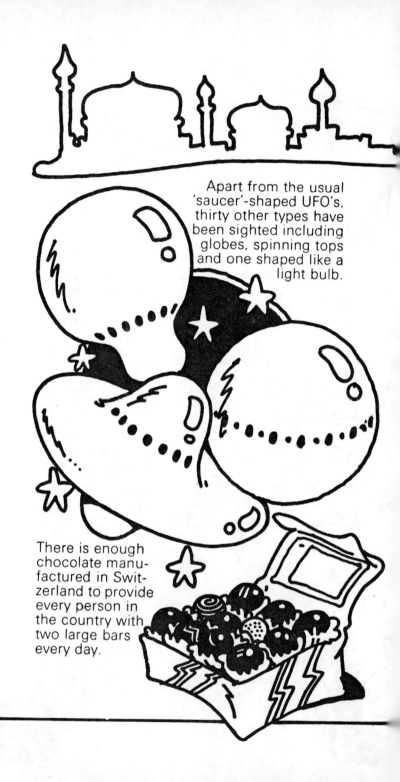

Apart from the usual 'saucer'-shaped UFO's, thirty other types have been sighted including globes, spinning tops and one shaped like a light bulb.

There is enough chocolate manufactured in Switzerland to provide every person in the country with two large bars every day.

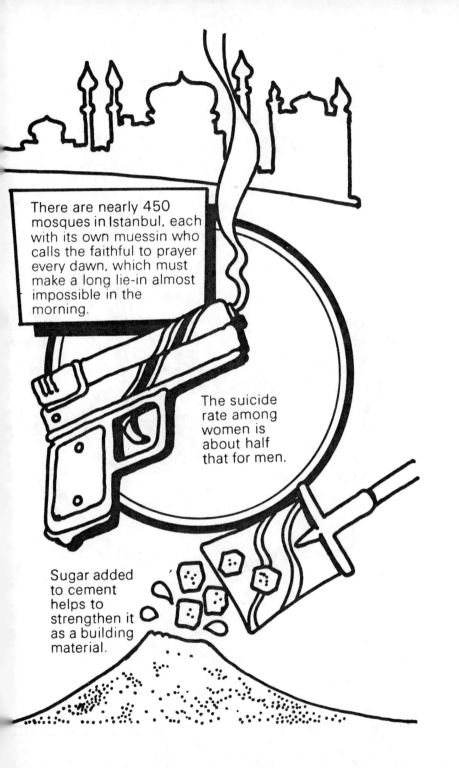

There are nearly 450 mosques in Istanbul, each with its own muessin who calls the faithful to prayer every dawn, which must make a long lie-in almost impossible in the morning.

The suicide rate among women is about half that for men.

Sugar added to cement helps to strengthen it as a building material.

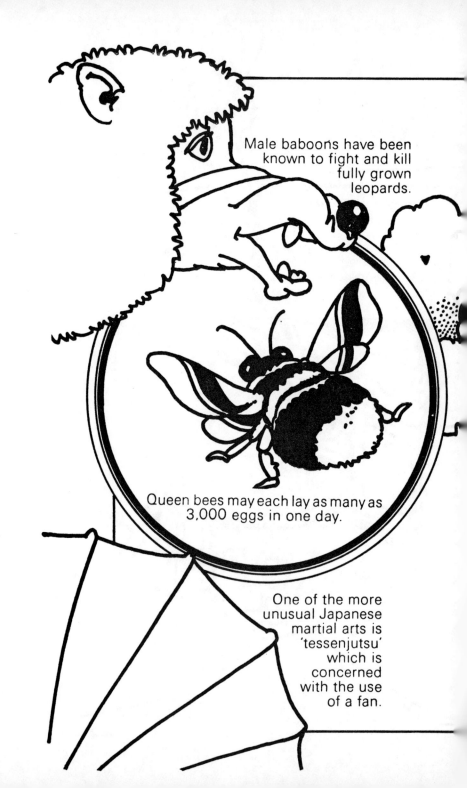

Male baboons have been known to fight and kill fully grown leopards.

Queen bees may each lay as many as 3,000 eggs in one day.

One of the more unusual Japanese martial arts is 'tessenjutsu' which is concerned with the use of a fan.

A silkworm can consume 86,000 times its own bodyweight in only 56 days.

80 per cent of all the species of freshwater fish that live on earth are found in the Amazon.

During the Stone Age it has been reckoned that there were as many left-handed people as right-handed people. By the Bronze Age this number had fallen by half and today about 5 per cent of the population are left-handed.

Every year about thirteen million working days are lost in Britain as a result of backache.

The designs adopted in medieval heraldry were based on magic symbols that used to be drawn on Roman shields to ward off the evil eye.

Since 1496 there have only been 233 years in which there has not been warfare somewhere in the civilised world.

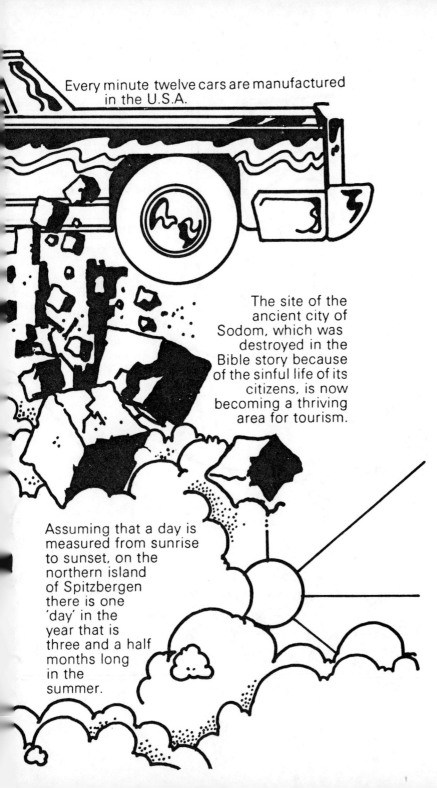

Every minute twelve cars are manufactured in the U.S.A.

The site of the ancient city of Sodom, which was destroyed in the Bible story because of the sinful life of its citizens, is now becoming a thriving area for tourism.

Assuming that a day is measured from sunrise to sunset, on the northern island of Spitzbergen there is one 'day' in the year that is three and a half months long in the summer.

During one period of political instability in Mexico three men were president in one day.

At the court of Louis XIV only the monarch and his queen were allowed to sit in chairs with arms.

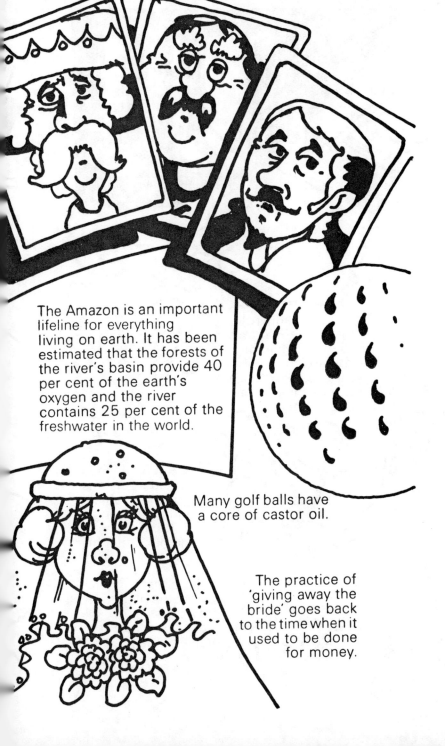

The Amazon is an important lifeline for everything living on earth. It has been estimated that the forests of the river's basin provide 40 per cent of the earth's oxygen and the river contains 25 per cent of the freshwater in the world.

Many golf balls have a core of castor oil.

The practice of 'giving away the bride' goes back to the time when it used to be done for money.

John Bunyan wrote most of the 'Pilgrim's Progress' while he was serving a twelve-year prison sentence for preaching without a licence.

One of Sir Joshua Reynolds' portraits shows the subject standing wearing a hat and carrying another under his arm.

Only about four per cent of the plants growing on earth are put to some form of use by man.

Despite being incorporated into the Christian faith, holly retained many of its pagan associations for hundreds of years after the druids had ceased to practice their art. In order to prevent themselves from becoming witches in the following year, girls used to tie sprigs of holly to their beds at Christmas.

The walls of Babylon were over 26m thick in some places.